HOW TO FORGIVE
A PRACTICAL GUIDE
LYNDA BEVAN

Loving Healing Press

How To Forgive: A Practical Guide
Book #5 in the 10-Step Empowerment Series
Copyright © 2011 by Lynda Bevan

Library of Congress Cataloging-in-Publication Data

Bevan, Lynda.
  How to forgive : a practical guide / by Lynda Bevan.
      p. cm. -- (10-step empowerment series ; 5)
  Includes bibliographical references and index.
  ISBN-13: 978-1-61599-031-3 (hbk. : alk. paper)
  ISBN-10: 1-61599-031-3 (hbk. : alk. paper)
  ISBN-13: 978-1-61599-030-6 (pbk. : alk. paper)
  ISBN-10: 1-61599-030-5 (pbk. : alk. paper)
  1. Forgiveness. I. Title.
  BF637.F67B48 2012
  155.9'2--dc22
                                    2011005970

Distributed by: Ingram Book Group, New Leaf Distributing,
Quality Books.

Published by:
Loving Healing Press
5145 Pontiac Trail
Ann Arbor, MI 48105-9627

info@LHPress.com   www.LovingHealing.com
Tollfree 888-761-6268   Fax 734-663-6861

What People Are Saying About
The 10-Step Empowerment Series

"Through the use of introspective questions, the book invites the reader to take a journey of self-examination in order to accept the loss and to reengage in life."

—Ian Landry, MA, MSW, Case Manager

"Bevan has real-life experience in the area of loss and "rebuilding" her life and self-esteem in the face of traumatic experiences such as being abandoned by a partner."

—Margaret M. Mustelier, PsyD

"Nowadays, there are too many books about adult loving relationships, but they usually are generic and abstract descriptions. This book is different because it moves to specificity and provides concrete steps to overcome a disrupting episode in our lives."

—Carlos J. Sanchez, MA, Family Therapist

"Lynda Bevan delivers what she promises in the title of the book: it is a practical guide and a no-nonsense approach. Her descriptions of the experiences are palpable."

—Chin Tao, LMFT

"This is a well thought out, useful little book that is an excellent guide for those recovering from a broken long-term relationship."

—Robert Rich, MSc, PhD, MAPS

"The book is studded with illuminating case studies and provides an excellent exposition of issues such as post-traumatic emotional responses, pre-trauma expectations, setting boundaries, forgiveness and acceptance, and the do's and don'ts of moving forward. A gem."

—Sam Vaknin, PhD
author *Malignant Self Love: Narcissism Revisited*

"Bevan provides practical steps to help a person begin the process of change, and during that process, to decide how the relationship will be affected, and whether to stay in the relationship, based on how your partner reacts to your new behaviors."

—Tyler R. Tichelaar, PhD
Author of *The Marquette Trilogy*

"This easy to relate to, solution-focused guide does not attempt to push an agenda; it simply provides a foundation of understanding along with the tools necessary to begin trusting one's own feelings again. Bevan dedicates great thought toward realistic problem solving approaches while maintaining a focus on safety, health, and growth."

—Erin M. Hudges, LCSW
Rebecca's Reads

"I truly feel that every individual who is dealing with issues of some form of jealousy will greatly benefit from reading *Life Without Jealousy* by Lynda Bevan. This includes people who are not jealous themselves but are being affected by others who are. Learning to understand it, overcome it, and gain effective new ways to communicate will greatly improve the quality of our lives."

Paige Lovitt
—*Reader Views*

When I was in college, I outlined all my lectures and readings so I could easily go back and study those points of importance without being bogged down with extraneous detail. That is what this book is - a detailed outline and explanation of how jealousy and envy in a relationship can be recognized and dealt with. It is a step-by-step guide into the psychology behind the emotions and a program to change them.

Enid Grabner,
—*Rebecca's Reads*

THE 10-STEP EMPOWERMENT SERIES

- Life After Your Lover Walks Out (2006)
- Life After Betrayal (2007)
- Stop Being Pushed Around! (2008)
- Life Without Jealousy (2009)
- How to Forgive (2011)

About our Series Editor, Robert Rich, PhD

Loving Healing Press is pleased to announce Robert Rich, PhD as Series Editor for the *10-Step Empowerment Series*. This exciting new series conveys practical guides written by seasoned therapists for solving real-life problems.

Robert Rich, MSc, PhD, MAPS, AASH is a highly experienced counseling psychologist. His website www.anxietyanddepression-help.com is a storehouse of helpful information for people suffering from anxiety and depression.

Bob is also a multiple award-winning writer of both fiction and non-fiction, and a professional editor. His writing is displayed at www.bobswriting.com. You are advised not to visit him there unless you have the time to get lost for a while.

Three of his books are tools for psychological self-help: *Anger and Anxiety: Be in charge of your emotions and control phobias*, *Personally Speaking: Single session email therapy*, and *Cancer: A personal challenge*. However, his philosophy and psychological knowledge come through in all his writing, which is perhaps why three of his books have won international awards, and he has won many minor prizes. Dr. Rich currently resides at Wombat Hollow in Australia.

Contents

1 | Understanding Forgiveness

I remember a line in a play I once acted in many years ago, and every now and then it pops into my mind: "To forgive is to overcome, and I have not forgiven you." I am really confused with this line as it suggests that unless you have overcome the issue and/or the person that you needed to forgive, then you have not forgiven that person. I am sure, like me, if someone has apologized to you for something that they said or did to you, you in return would reply, "Apology accepted, don't worry, no problem," and life would carry on regardless. It isn't that simple though, is it? Life doesn't just carry on regardless. These deeds, large or small, that have hurt you emotionally are stored in your mind, and when a situation occurs that is similar to past deeds, you begin to have doubts as to whether you have forgiven that person, because you certainly have not forgotten it if it pops up in your mind when a similar situation occurs. This issue begs many questions. One is, "If you haven't forgotten the deed, does that mean that you haven't forgiven either?"

This book will identify the many aspects and meanings of the word "forgiveness" and will attempt to enable you to understand exactly how being able to forgive someone is a basic, essential, necessary process in your life. The focus of this book is "forgiveness in adult relationships." Forgiveness is such an important word, and the action that follows the word is humbling if it is said and done genuinely and sincerely. The person apologizing will feel vulnerable and embarrassed.

Ask yourself:
- Have you asked someone/your partner to forgive you?
- Have you really wanted to be forgiven by that person/your partner?
- Have you only asked to be forgiven in order to keep your partner happy so that person believes that he/she is still in control of the relationship?
- Have you found it easy to ask for forgiveness?
- Have you asked for forgiveness so many times that you now feel devalued and lacking self-worth?
- Have you paid the price of repeatedly asking for forgiveness from your partner even when you have done no wrong?
- Have you lost the love you had for your partner through accepting blame and because you have been expected to ask for forgiveness?

I will explore these questions and give some simple explanations in Step 2.

To Forgive, What Does it Mean?

"Forgive" according to *Webster's New World Dictionary*, means: "to give up resentment against or the desire to punish; pardon; to overlook an offense; to cancel a debt."

If you are unable to forgive, you are unable to "move on" in your life. When you believe that you cannot forgive someone, it will eat you up and destroy the relationship you have with your partner/family member/friend. It will also destroy the relationship you have with yourself. It is not healthy to keep resentment bottled up inside you. Not being able to forgive someone means that you are continually tied to the person you should have forgiven. Many people may require forgiveness by you, and if this is the case then your negative thought process will have totally taken control over you, and you will be stuck in the negative groove of your own making. When you look at "forgiveness" from this viewpoint you will see that it is essential, for the sake of your mental health, to challenge your current thoughts and work through the process of identifying the cause of your unforgiving attitude. This is to release your negative thought process and replace it with a positive one that will enable you to regain self-control and healthy power now and in future situations. More about how to engage in changing your negative thought processes to positive thought processes is given later on in this book.

> "To err is human; to forgive, Divine."
> Alexander Pope, *An Essay on Criticism*

Here are some examples of issues that require forgiveness:

- People spreading malicious lies aimed at casting you in a bad light
- People who have been emotionally abusive toward you
- People who have been physically violent toward you (if this is the case, your life may be in danger—get help.)
- If you have been embarrassed by your partner
- If you have been humiliated by your partner
- If you have caused someone/your partner's self-esteem to drop significantly
- If you are holding on to a grudge against a past partner
- If you are holding on to a grudge against your parents
- If you are holding a grudge because you have been conned regarding financial issues
- If you are holding on to issues with siblings (rivalry)
- If you are holding on to jealousy issues
- If you cannot forgive your partner for having an affair
- If you are holding a grudge against your step-children (who haven't accepted you)

- If you believe your partner is more successful than you are and are holding a grudge with your partner because of this
- If you believe your partner is more popular than you are and you continually feel marginalized.

This list is endless and will be different for each of you. Let's take a look at each of the above.

When Malicious Lies are Spread about You

This is a particularly ugly scenario and one that makes you feel that you can't trust anyone. You have to ask, "Why do people talk in this way behind my back?'

Here are some examples of when this happens...

- When someone is jealous of you
- When someone doesn't know you and makes wrong assumptions
- When someone wants what you've got
- When someone is unkind
- When someone takes an instant dislike to you
- When someone doesn't know how to approach you and then assumes that you are unapproachable
- When someone believes that you don't like them
- When someone feels intimated by you
- When someone believes you have ignored them
- When there is a misunderstanding between you
- When there is a quarrel between you.
- When someone believes that you have done something that they disapprove of.
- When you let someone down
- When you are found out
- When someone believes that you have talked about them behind their back

- When you don't take sides and you are "sent to Coventry" (shunned by one or both sides).

Whatever the reason, the outcome is distasteful and, sometimes, difficult to repair. The best way to repair the problem is to face it head on and tackle the person or people who you believe are talking about you. This needn't be done in a confrontational, aggressive way. A cool, calm approach in these circumstances is always the best way.

An example of how to approach this is:

You say: "I've heard some terrible things you've said about me, and I find it hard to believe that you would talk about me in this way behind my back. Please tell me what you've heard and give me the opportunity of clarifying the situation for you." If you make the statement or ask the question in this way, you will not aggravate or upset the person and they will react in the same manner.

Emotional Abuse

Someone on the receiving end of emotional abuse often does not know that they are being abused. They become so familiar and accepting of the way they are being treated that they fail to identify that they are being abused. It is hard to understand and accept that you are being emotionally abused, and even more confusing is how you stop it.

Here are some examples of emotional abuse:

- You are intimidated by your partner
- You are bullied by your partner
- You are interrogated by your partner
- You are constantly ignored by your partner
- You are verbally threatened by your partner
- You are ridiculed by your partner
- You are undermined by your partner
- You are nagged (persecuted) by your partner
- You are not allowed to make a decision for yourself

- You are controlled by your partner
- You are manipulated by your partner
- You are denied help from your partner
- You feel the necessity to hide things from your partner in fear of their reaction
- You live on a tight budget that is controlled by your partner.

All of the above are forms of emotional abuse. There are more—I am sure you can add to this list. In order to change the way you are treated by your partner, you have to make a conscious decision to make changes in yourself. Small changes in your behavior, reactions and speech will force a change in the way your partner responds to you. It is necessary to make very small changes in your behavior at first and see the difference this makes to your partner's response. You need to forgive your partner first and then begin a process of small changes to shift the power in your relationship with your partner.

Physical Violence

I personally would not continue living with someone who is physically violent toward me. No one deserves to be treated in this way. It is the act of a coward. If you are in this situation, my advice is to get out of the relationship as quickly as possible. I have met people who have forgiven their partner who has been physically violent toward them, but I have yet to meet someone who has managed to curb his/her anger and stop being violent permanently. They might succeed for a while, but eventually the old bad habit returns.

Remember you don't have to put up with this behavior. You always have the option of separating/divorcing. However, John Gottman's research shows there are two types of physical abusers. Type 1 abusers are likely to respond to attempts at separation with murder, so it's not necessarily that simple. The woman needs to plan the separation very carefully. If you have had violence done to you or received the threat of violence, you are advised to contact your nearest Domestic Violence Support center for advice before acting (see Appendix).

Embarrassment, Humiliation, & Self-Esteem

Embarrassed by Your Partner

It is so cringe-making to be made a fool of by your partner. You feel stupid, and the reaction from people around at that time varies from feeling sorry for you to criticizing you for allowing this to happen. *Why do you allow it to happen?* You allow it to happen because it makes for an easier life in the short term. It is only when you have experienced this type of behavior in a relationship that you can understand the "peace at any price" method. If you react and retaliate to your partner's remark, World War III will erupt before your very eyes. The "peace at any price method" only comes about by experiencing the verbal onslaught of anger and then seeing the demonic look on the face of your partner when he/she is challenged by you. In order to forgive your partner, it will be necessary for you to believe that your partner knows he/she is wrong by embarrassing you. If you suspect that they are just cajoling you, then rest assured your partner will resort to this type of behavior again in the not too distant future. There are ways around this situation that involve you making small changes in your behavior that will eventually stop your partner embarrassing you.

Humiliated by Your Partner

Humiliation is doled out by your partner so that he/she can be perceived as being better and/or cleverer than you are. Some people use humiliation as a weapon to get their own way. These people ridicule every comment or suggestion you make. The result of this constant criticizing is that your self-esteem will disappear and you will become beholden to your partner to tell you how to think, behave and speak.

Humiliation, ridicule, criticizing, and ignoring result in low self-esteem, low self-worth and no confidence. Forgiving someone who is treating you badly is a huge hurdle to overcome.

Causing Your Partner to Lose Self-Esteem

If you have controlled your partner so much to cause him/her to lose their self-esteem, then you are guilty of behaving in a destructive way to another human being. Taking away someone's self-esteem is also taking away that person's self-respect. No one has a right to do this. A healthy relationship is based on two people having an equal say. If you are the person who is guilty of this behavior, then you need to ask for forgiveness and genuinely mean it. If your partner loves you enough and is prepared to give you a second chance, then consider yourself lucky you have found someone who is prepared to go that extra mile for you in the hope that you will not repeat this behavior.

Holding Grudges Against Family

Past Partners

What can you gain by holding a long-term grudge against an ex? All you are accomplishing is holding yourself back from living a positive, healthy life. Your ex-partner is probably unaware that you are carrying a grudge against them and are having a good time in their new life without you. You, however, are harboring bad thoughts and will become bitter and revengeful. Carrying the burden of a grudge will destroy any new relationship you will have in the future. You will bring excess negative baggage into any new relationship and will probably resort to punishing your new partner for the sins of your ex-partner. Let the grudge go. It isn't worth hanging on to.

Ruminating over unrealistic ideals such as "fairness" or "justice" will get you nowhere. It is doing no harm to your ex-partner and a great load of harm to you and your new relationship. Women who have been abandoned by men will feel bitter and resentful for a while after a breakup—it is part of the grieving process in any relationship. It would appear that men are able to move on quicker than women. Not being able to let go becomes a problem when someone is stuck in that particular phase of the grieving process. When this happens, it is advisable to seek professional help to forgive your ex and assist you in "moving on."

Step-Children

When you become involved with someone with children, you will have to accept that the child's/children's needs come first. You can never expect a parent (male or female) to put you before their offspring. It takes time for children to accept that their Mom or Dad has someone new in their life, so care and caution are important in order to give the right message to the child/children, which is: "I am not going to take Mommy or Daddy away from you, and I want to involve you in this relationship."

Your Parents

Some of the people who enter therapy believe that they are the way they are because of something that happened in their childhood. This might indeed be the case. However, if this is the case, once it has been identified and worked through, the person should be able to forgive their parents and let go of the pain and hurt and move on. Stop procrastinating. Become a new you and leave the past behind.

Siblings

Conflict between siblings can be about childhood incidents that the siblings have brought into adulthood. Resentments and hostilities can become especially difficult to overcome if the situation has resulted in the siblings not speaking to each other. Usually, conflict regarding past issues can be overcome by the people involved having calm discussions to clear up any misunderstandings that occurred way back then. Sometimes these issues from the past are best left there with no post mortem to unravel complex emotions that have been either enlarged over the years or dimmed with forgetfulness. A decision to "move on" regardless could be the best option in many cases. Another area of conflict between siblings occurs after the death of one or both parents. "Money is the root of all evil," and especially so after a bereavement. Squabbles over who gets what are the source of many fall outs between siblings.

When a Partner Misuses Your Money

- Have you been duped?
- Do you feel foolish in believing what your partner tells you?
- Have you forgiven your partner?
- Do you believe that your partner might treat you in this way again?

Ask yourself all these questions and many more before you decide to forgive your partner and stay in the relationship. If your partner has "pulled the wool over your eyes" and manipulated your joint finances, you must be sure that it won't happen again before you continue in the relationship. It seems obvious to keep an eye on your bank and credit card statement. Another suggestion is to take over the control of the financial budget for a while. Doing this will help you to understand exactly what your partner has done, and you will be able to sleep nights knowing that you are in charge of your joint finances for the time being at least.

Holding on to Jealousy Issues

Jealousy is at the core of resentment, guilt, hostility and revenge. Jealousy is always lurking to bite you on your backside when you least expect it. Jealousy will find a way of messing with your emotions and causing serious relationship mayhem. The best way to tackle jealousy is head on. By that I mean ,confront whoever you believe has caused you to become jealous. This confrontation shouldn't be done aggressively. You can reach a satisfactory outcome by calmly approaching the person and tell them about the problem you are facing. Some people who are behaving jealously do so because they have a fear of being alone, unloved and rejected by their partner. In this particular case, support from their partner is essential to allay these destructive feelings.

If you are experiencing jealousy, I would urge you to always think logically about the situation you are jealous about. Don't be tempted to assume stuff. Don't add on to situations that you feel are aimed against you. Try to stop analyzing conversations and body language. Just accept things as they really are. Lastly, forgive yourself when you are jealous and behaving badly. Learn by your past mistakes of jealousy issues and don't repeat them. Don't keep things to yourself. Share your thoughts with your partner, family, or friends. Ask people to be objective and tell you the truth. Some people will tell you what they believe you want to hear. This is unacceptable and can make the situation worse and make you look a fool. I cover this subject in depth in my book *Life Without Jealousy: A Practical Guide.*

After Your Partner has Cheated on You

This situation is difficult to overcome. When the trust between a couple is poisoned by one of you having an affair, it will take quite some time to reestablish the trust in your relationship. It can be done, however, but it will be necessary for you both to set new ground rules that your future relationship will be based on. The partner who has been betrayed will be reluctant to "move on" in the relationship until they are satisfied that their partner is truly sorry and repentant of their deeds. It might be necessary for the betrayer to pay a penance to compensate for the betrayal. Patience, understanding and communication are the keys in order to overcome jealousy due to betrayal. I cover this subject in depth in my book *Life After Betrayal: A Practical Guide*.

Envious of a Successful Partner

You may think that this scenario is quite rare, when in fact it is the opposite as more and more women are occupying senior posts in the public, corporate and statutory (schools and hospitals) sectors. I know I am generalizing when I say that most men are ego-driven, but when this is the case and their partners are earning more money and have more power in the workplace, this can cause rivalry between a couple with each of them vying for first place with regard to having more power in the relationship. Historically, men were the bread-winners in the family, but this is not necessarily so in today's culture. It has being recognized that women are starting families much later, which further highlights that not only are women playing a vital role in the marketplace, but they are also reluctant to surrender to domesticity too early in their life.

Valuing yourself by someone else's standards

If you only value and validate yourself through your work, this leaves an empty vacuum within you that needs to be filled. But, you are more than just a workhorse. You are more than just a provider. You are a unique individual who has a multi-faceted personality that you must recognize and own. With modern day stresses and pressures, it is difficult to find the space during the course of your working week to come up with ideas on how to capitalize on your individual personal identity. Ideally, time should be allocated to allow you to explore what you want from your life quite apart from your work. You should ask yourself, "Who am I behind my professional mask? Do I know myself?" Do you feel vulnerable and sensitive when you are not at work?

If you are holding a grudge against your partner because he/she is more successful than you are, then these are examples of some of the questions you should be asking yourself. If you are thinking in this way, it says more about your fears and insecurities than it does about your partner. Grudges start the rot in a relationship and should be addressed as soon as possible. How you value yourself is central to the success of your relationship. If you don't believe in yourself and you don't have a positive self-image, how can you expect your partner to value you?

When you feel marginalized by partner who is "popular"

Successful men are usually popular people. Here are some possible reasons:

- Wealth: money is attractive
- Influence: others may covet their power
- Charm: charisma
- Behavior: appearing to do everything right
- Cleverness: always ready with counter-measures
- Interesting: gift of the gab, never at a loss for words.

Unfortunately, most of the successful men I have met are rude, over-bearing, arrogant manipulators. They use their position and power to get what they want at any cost. They are above being challenged by people they work with and are seldom confronted with opposition to the suggestions they make. This is a sweeping statement about powerful men, so I should also say that I know powerful men who are kind, generous, and sensitive to the needs of others.

What are you going to do about it?

Here are some examples of your negative options:

- Grudgingly accept the situation as it is and do nothing
- Intimidate your partner whenever possible
- Ridicule your partner, possibly in front of people you don't know very well

- Ignore what your partner says and blithely carry on regardless
- Make a fool of him/her at every opportunity
- Be amused that he/she is well received and liked, and smile to yourself when you imagine how cranky and difficult he/she is at home
- Be aware that there are predators who will misunderstand your partner's motives and will think that your partner is fancying them.

Or...

Here are some examples of your positive options:
- Be proud that your partner is hospitable and warm
- Celebrate your partner's popularity and remember that you chose this person as your partner in life, so it reflects well on you that you did this
- Observe and learn how your partner engages people and emulate his/her behavior
- Decide to train yourself to be engaging in social circles.

> "Any situation that you find yourself in is an outward reflection of your inner state of beingness."
>
> Ascended Master El Morya

2 | "Forgive and Forget?"

I've often heard this phrase. Let's examine the concept of forgiving and forgetting in an adult relationship.

What does forgiving in a relationship mean?

Here are some examples for the forgiver:

Forgiving in a relationship means...

- That you accept that no one is perfect
- That you are not prepared to hold grudges
- That you genuinely believe that your partner feels remorse and is sincerely sorry for his/her words and or actions
- That you have accepted your partner's explanation
- That your partner has accepted the blame and owned up to whatever it is they have said or done, and that you believe that your partner will learn from his/her mistakes and will not repeat the deed in the future
- That you will trust your partner and are prepared to continue with the relationship without putting barriers in place
- That you can openly display of the love you feel for him/her
- That you let go of grudges, lies and disappointment.

What is the difference between forgiving and forgetting?

Here are some examples for the forgiver:

Forgetting is...
- Being able to put the past behind you and no longer let this issue form a barrier between you and your partner
- No longer referring to the issue that caused the problem
- Never throwing jibes and comments at your partner about what took place at that time
- Being able to let go of hurt and anger and not allowing these emotions to erode your relationship
- Allowing your relationship to strengthen in the long-term
- Enabling your partner to re-establish a loving relationship with you
- Adhering to a joint "plan" that re-establishes basic behavior and ground rules in the relationship
- Letting go any thoughts of revenge.

What do you believe forgiving and forgetting means?

Here are some examples to help you:

If you ask forgiveness, you want it understood that...
- You don't want to speak about the incident again
- You don't want your partner to interpret this as a sign that you are feeble
- You don't want your partner to use this against you
- It has been difficult for you to do and are only doing so because you believe the relationship is worth you both trying harder to make it work.

In **Step 1**, I suggested a list of questions you should ask yourself. In this step, I am encouraging you to answer these questions. Take as long as you like, but answer them honestly. I will assist you in this exercise by offering an explanation of each question.

I will repeat the questions I mentioned in Step 1 and will give an explanation for each of them:

1. Have you asked someone/your partner to forgive you?
2. Have you really wanted to be forgiven by that person/ your partner?
3. Have you only asked to be forgiven in order to keep your partner happy so they continue to believe that they are still in control of the relationship?
4. Have you found it easy to ask for forgiveness?
5. Have you asked for forgiveness so many times that you now feel de-valued and lacking self-worth?
6. Have you paid the price of repeatedly asking for forgiveness from your partner even when you have done no wrong?
7. Have you lost the love you had for your partner through accepting blame and because you have been expected to ask for forgiveness?

Let's look at the first question:

1. Have you asked someone/your partner to forgive you?

If you answer "yes" to this question, then you will know how difficult and embarrassing it is to acknowledge to your partner the fact that you believe and own that you have made a mistake. This gesture requires courage and honesty. If you are or were able to ask for forgiveness, the non-verbal communication you are giving your partner is that you won't make the same mistake again. If you are not genuine in asking for forgiveness, then you will be asking your partner for forgiveness because you know that is what is needed for your partner to forget the problem. In other words you are lying to your partner for your own hidden agenda.

In order to move on and have a healthy relationship, it is vital that you mean what you say and that you are not just saying the words to "shut your partner up."

If you are honest and really mean what you say, how did it feel asking for forgiveness?

Here are some examples of how it may feel to ask for forgiveness:

- Humiliating
- Embarrassing
- Humbling
- Confrontational
- Empowering
- That you are trusting and have blind faith in the process of forgiveness
- Childish that at your age you need to ask for forgiveness
- Like you are emotionally cleansing your mind
- A relief to get it off your chest
- Like letting go of something bad
- Like the beginning of a fresh start.

Has your partner/someone ever thrown something back at you that you previously asked forgiveness for?

If you have experienced this act of betrayal of trust, then you will be disinclined to be honest and own up in the future. Trust is an essential element in moving on from asking for forgiveness, and having something thrown back in your face after thinking you were forgiven is the last thing you would expect your partner to do.

If you have experienced this act of betrayal, how did/does it make you feel? Here are some examples:

It makes you feel....

- Betrayed
- Worthless
- Foolish
- Like you will never apologise or ask for forgiveness again
- Embarrassed, particularly if it is done in front of other people

- Hurt
- Angry
- Vengeful
- Resentful

As you can see, this list could be endless. These are all powerful feelings that will be imprinted in your memory and will stop you from being honest and owning up to anything else in the future.

In the forgiving and forgetting stage, what are the thoughts and emotions you are aware of?

Here are some examples to assist you:

The thoughts provoke you to...

1. look at yourself
2. look at your partner
3. value your relationship
4. be anxious about appearing vulnerable to your partner.

It is difficult to look at yourself, your behavior, attitude, actions and speech, but this is integral to coming to terms with identifying what exactly needs to change.

Let's take a look at each of these statements.

A. The thoughts provoke you to look at yourself

Some people do not want to look at their own behavior. Others believe that they are always right whatever the circumstances. To forgive and forget, you will accept that you must look at the part you have played in the scenario that has unfolded. If you cannot see that you had a part to play and acknowledge what that part was, you will be unable to move on from this stuck stage. It is the height of vanity and arrogance to believe that you are always totally blameless.

Furthermore, there is no point to blame, shame and guilt. Consider where responsibility lies. If the other person is 100% responsible for the problem, then I am helpless: I can only rely on the other person to make changes. If I can identify what I have contributed to the problem, then I have the power to make changes.

B. The thoughts provoke you to look at your partner

Most people find it easier to look at the behavior of others than to look at their own behavior. You are probably too ready to criticize someone else than to criticize yourself. If I asked you to make a list of your partner's bad points, I am sure that you could recall and identify them very quickly. You will find it easier to pinpoint the role your partner has played in the scenario and will blank out or block your role in the scenario. Love is being able to love your partner despite his/her faults.

C. The thoughts provoke you to reassess and to value your relationship

When you are able to acknowledge and accept your role in the scenario and also accept that you have played a significant part in creating and continuing the problem, then you will see that you must take partial responsibility and accountability for the way things have turned out. The negative side of acceptance is that you might feel foolish that you have jumped to conclusions too soon and interpreted what your partner has said or done wrongly. The positive side of acceptance is that you are behaving as a mature adult in finding out and accepting that you did have a role to play and that you are prepared to accept the responsibility of your errors.

D. The thoughts provoke you to be anxious about appearing vulnerable to your partner

If you feel vulnerable due to accepting responsibility for your actions in the scenario, it will be because accepting responsibility is a new thing for you to do, and the more you understand yourself and your interactions with others/your partner, the easier it will be for you to do this.

2. Have you really wanted to be forgiven by your partner?

You should only ask for forgiveness from your partner if you genuinely believe that you were partly to blame. Before asking for forgiveness, it is essential that you look at your role in the situation and are able to identify where you went wrong in your interaction with your partner regarding the conflicting issue. If you are unable to do this, asking for forgiveness is useless in the moving on stage as there will be no moving on for either of you when this happens, as the future will be based on a lie.

3. Have you only asked for forgiveness in order to keep your partner happy so they continue to believe that they are still in control of the relationship?

Ask yourself, "How many times have I asked for forgiveness just to keep my partner happy?" and "Why do I do this?" Many women I have counseled have used this strategy on a regular basis. It's the "peace at any price" method. When you adopt this strategy, what you are actually doing is storing up the conflicting issues in your memory box, and continuing doing this will result in you becoming resentful and bitter toward your partner.

4. Have you found it easy to ask for forgiveness?

When you ask for forgiveness it is natural to feel vulnerable and foolish. The truth is, however, that saying you are sorry and asking for forgiveness strengthens your mind, re-energizes your soul and empowers you. You will feel humility perhaps for the first time, and while this experience highlights your weakness, it will be beneficial in the long term by strengthening your character.

5. Have you asked for forgiveness so many times that you now feel devalued and lacking in self-worth?

If your partner is in control of the relationship and expects you to be servile to him/her, you will feel disempowered and lacking in self-worth. It's a vicious circle isn't it? Your partner expects you to react in a particular way and you try to fulfill your obligations by complying to his/her wishes, but when do you stop reacting and using this disabling method? To restate this question, "How can you begin to look at each other and your relationship in a more positive light?" Taking change a small step at a time will help you change your automatic reactions.

Here are some ideas and options you could try:

- Putting each other first, stop making it all about you.
- Change your usual pattern of what you do when you are in conflict with your partner. Do you run to a friend or a family member for support? Try not to do this and instead remove yourself from the room and occupy yourself with some trivial task.

  By doing this you are sending several non-verbal messages to your partner that you (a) are not fazed by the conflict and do not need someone else to support you; (b) you are confident enough to deal with yourself; (c) you don't put the problem and the conflict high on your support agenda. This will have an effect on the way your partner behaves and it should draw you closer to each other.

- Devise a structure to get back your self-worth. Join a gym, take a class to learn a new skill, go out shopping with friends, do anything that will empower you, but nothing that will distance yourself any further from your partner.

- During arguments, stop speaking and ask for a hug. Your partner might be shocked and refuse to give you one, but if you are persuasive I am sure that you will get one eventually. Doing this will temporarily disarm your partner.

- Aim for better communication between the two of you. Tell your partner that you don't like arguing and would rather talk things through rationally and calmly.

- Ask your partner how you could support him/her and tell your partner how he/she can support you.
- Try and spend quality time together doing things, e.g., a walk, movies, meeting up with friends. By doing these things you will both be distracted from the conflict you are experiencing, and also it will stop either of you needing support from others.
- Re-make a commitment to each other.

6. Have you paid the price of repeatedly asking for forgiveness from your partner even when you have done no wrong?

If you have engaged in this interaction, you will have paid the price by experiencing your personality diminishing, your assertiveness evaporating, your behavior becoming pathetic, and you will be unable to make a decision because you are treading on eggshells around your partner. All these things are a high price to pay particularly when you believe that you have done nothing wrong. This continued behavior on your part will make you resentful of your partner, which will create a distance between you that will be difficult to fix.

Please take into consideration that your behavior only serves to reinforce your partner's power over you and in your relationship. This is the "peace at any price" method of communication. The bottom line is that you are actually colluding with your partner, ensuring that he/she stays the same. It is tempting in the first instance to adopt this method during conflict, but it cannot be sustained over a long period of time without bitterness eroding the relationship. Continuing this practice can also result in you becoming depressed.

7. Have you lost the love you had for your partner through accepting blame and because you have been expected to ask for forgiveness?

Unfortunately this is the consequence of an unrealistic expectation your partner has placed on you and which you have succumbed to. Controlling someone is a risky business

for the controller in that the relationship will only succeed on
his/her terms. Eventually the servile partner will "wake up
and smell the coffee" and will want to stop behaving and
reacting in this way. That's when the trouble really starts and
the nastiness begins. The years you have spent hiding the
bitterness and resentment will explode and will be difficult to
contain. It will take a solid relationship and a lot of love to
overcome this situation.

Here are some examples on how to overcome this situation:

The servile partner must...

- Let go past resentments and hostility
- Have "blind faith" in moving on from this place
- Release fears that he/she has hung on to
- Take risks to overcome the situation
- Work through the anger they are feeling (either with
  their partner, a trusted friend or a therapist)
- Practice and be comfortable with open and honest
  communication
- Learn how to trust
- Start believing that everyone has the capacity to change
- Recognize and acknowledge their part in the conflict
  situations.

Here are some examples for the Controlling partner to adopt:

The controller must...

- Learn to accept that his/her partner is an equal and has
  a right to be heard and have their say
- Allow his/her partner to grow in the relationship
- Allow sufficient time to elapse in order for the servile
  partner to readjust into his/her new role
- Let go of his/her fears and need to control the
  relationship
- Learn to take a risk and allow his/her partner to take
  the lead in the relationship some of the time

- Learn to develop trust in his/her partner
- Realize that the relationship is not a competition; no-one is the winner in a loving relationship
- Learn what their part is in conflict situations and be prepared to look at their thoughts, actions and behavior patterns
- Have support and/or guidance from a trusted friend, their partner or a professional therapist.

This is a huge block to overcome for both partners and the good news is that it can be done.

Another exercise that could be useful at this stage of development is to ask these questions:

Who is responsible for...

- My behavior in the conflict?
- My reaction in the conflict?
- My feelings in the conflict?
- Me being stuck in the conflict?

When you are able to answer these questions honestly, you can move on to the next stage in the exercise.

Ask yourself:

- How can I put this conflict behind me?
- How can I forgive my partner?
- How can I make sure that I won't be hurt in future conflicts if I let go of control?
- What reward do I get for blaming my partner for the feelings I experience?

"If we really want to love, we must learn how to forgive."

—Mother Theresa

3 | What Happens If You Can't Forget?

Of course, we don't mean "forget" in the sense of being physically unable to remember an event. "Forget" in terms of forgiveness means that a reminder of such an incident will not trigger unwanted feelings of rage, sadness, anxiety, or low spirits. It also means that we cease actively reminding ourselves, arming ourselves against threats which are in the past.

What happens if you cannot forgive and forget?

Here are some examples of what can occur for the person being asked for forgiveness:

If you cannot forgive and forget, you will...

- Continue to cause yourself serious emotional hurt and pain
- Continue to search for ways of revenge
- Become bitter
- Withdraw from your partner and place barriers between you so that your partner cannot hurt you anymore
- Remain angry. To internalize anger may result in having panic attacks, anxiety and depression. Your immune system willl be compromised and you may develop heart disease or cancer.
- Stop growing and developing emotionally

- Become secretive, develop hidden agendas against your partner and subconsciously plan a campaign to punish your partner
- Use up your power and energy and be constantly tired and lethargic.

...and then some. From this list you will see that being able to forgive and forget is a vital ingredient in order to have a healthy relationship with yourself and with your partner.

What are your beliefs if you cannot forgive and forget?

Here are some examples if you are the person being asked for forgiveness:

You believe that...

- The way you were treated should not be forgiven at any price
- You need to protect yourself and will never allow anyone else to be close to you
- You will never trust anyone ever again
- Forgiveness is a sign of weakness
- You might forgive but will never forget
- Your partner does not warrant your forgiveness because he/she has not compensated you for their misdeed
- To forgive and forget is losing your power to your partner
- To forgive and forget you must seek revenge
- Only God can forgive and forget
- To forgive and to forget gives your partner permission to abuse you again.

If you can't forgive and forget, what will happen to your relationship?

Here are some examples:

If you can't forgive and forget, you will...
- Begin hating your partner
- Withdraw from your partner
- Become angry
- Seek revenge
- Continually throw the past at your partner
- Become anxious
- Become depressed
- Become suspicious
- Become hostile
- Become petty
- End your relationship.

What do you need to do to forgive and forget?

Here are some examples:

To forgive and forget, you will need to...
- Let go of your fears
- Let go your feeling of insecurity
- Let go your feeling of wanting to control your partner
- Let go your hurts and disappointments
- Let go your judgmental attitude
- Let go your hostility and anger
- Let go your safety net and start taking risks
- Learn to trust your partner
- Trust yourself
- Develop coping strategies to enable the process of change
- Be honest with yourself and with your partner
- Communicate with your partner
- Acknowledge the part you have played to bring the relationship to this level
- Confront problems in a calm, logical manner

- Let go the irrational thoughts and beliefs that make up your negative thought processes.

> "Love is an act of endless forgiveness."
> —Peter Ustinov

These are just some of the things that you must learn to face, work through and dismiss from your thought processes. In order to move on it will be helpful to do the following exercise so you can identify and unblock barriers:

Ask yourself...

- Who was responsible for my reaction to the incident?
- Who was responsible for my feelings about the incident?
- Who was responsible for my inability to forgive the person(s) involved?
- Who is responsible for my inability to forget this incident?
- How can I forgive the person(s) involved?
- How can I put this incident behind me?
- How can I forgive myself for being dependent on others for feelings of being worthwhile and good?
- How can I avoid being so hurt when something like this happens again?
- What do I gain by blaming others for my feelings?

When you are able to answer all these questions, you will be better placed to move on. Learning how to forgive and forget is a daunting task for those people who have held on to hurt and pain and for anyone who holds his/her partner or someone else responsible for them in their life. Constant harping on about the past and the way you were treated is sometimes used as an excuse for not accepting responsibility and accountability for the person you are now. You can't live for the rest of your life blaming your parents or past relationships for the way you have turned out. You can create the person you want to become. So do it. Get on with it. Stop prevaricating and move on.

In order to move on successfully, you should construct and develop both long-term and short-term strategies that will enable this process. We'll look at three long-term strategies first:

1. Take personal responsibility for the choices you have made so far in your life. Take no blame for this. You are where you are and that cannot be changed. Don't carry the baggage of wrong decisions in the "here and now" because doing this will hold you back.

To keep moving forward, focus on the future and on making your life the way you want it to be. Don't sit back and be a "victim" waiting for good things to happen. They won't.

Try constructing a screenplay of the character you *want to be*. This is of necessity limited to what can be seen and heard; remember inner stuff like feelings and thoughts in a performance cannot be captured by camera and microphone.

2. Recognize the blocks in your life. Blocks are things that "get on your nerves." While some of these blocks appear small and insignificant, together they are a formidable energy sapping device. Blocks are anything from a door that doesn't shut properly to a job you hate. The more blocks you are able to recognize, the more tired and sapped of energy you will feel. When you recognize and list your blocks and decide to do something about them, you will become much more aware of your current situation and you will gain energy, become empowered, raise the quality of your life, and become self-confident. You are now starting your journey of self development, which will enrich your life and your partner's life.

3. Create a vision for the future. What is a vision? A vision is what you want and where you want to be. Your vision is the difference between where you are now and where you want to be.

In order to fulfill your vision you have to take responsibility for yourself and your life. You cannot follow the same path—you have to change course and build your dream.

As outlined in the 1st element, you must take responsibility for yourself and your actions. To turn your vision into reality requires patience, durability, strength and a willingness to follow through despite possible and probable setbacks. Someone who takes responsibility is someone you can look up to and admire, not just for their achievements but for their attitude and the way they handle themselves, situations and other people.

Devise a short-term strategy

What is a short-term strategy? It is a short-term plan of achievable goals.

In order to be effective your goals need to be:
- Realistic
- Attainable
- Measurable
- Prioritized according to:
  o What must be done
  o What may be done
  o What must not be done.

Realistic Goals

By realistic I mean achievable by your own efforts. It is pointless setting yourself unrealistic goals. Set believable goals and save yourself a hard time. Break your goals down into small achievable targets. You will be able to achieve your bigger goals if you work on achieving smaller targets. It is very important to make your goals as realistic and achievable as you can.

People Who Substitute Relationships for Goals

There are some among us who obsesss over relationships as the only worthwhile goal. In order to proceed with a strategy, you have to take responsibility for yourself and your life. Your success in achieving your goals depends entirely on you. You wouldn't be reading this book if you already had everything you wanted in life, were confident within yourself, happy, fulfilled and contented. So, do you believe enough in yourself and in what you can do to achieve your goals? Self-doubt and fear are huge obstacles you will come across on your way to a successful outcome. Self-doubt creeps up on you unsuspectingly. One day you might be confident, assertive and capable, and then almost overnight it would appear you have become less so.

What happened? You lost your power and went from an independent being to someone unable to survive without being in a relationship. It doesn't even have to be a good relationship now. Any relationship will do to validate you. You become dependent on another person/your partner to make you feel OK. You feel worthless without having a lover/partner/husband. This situation occurs when you lose focus of yourself. The "in love syndrome" fools you into believing you have everything that your heart desires. Being in love is an excuse to divert your attention from what you really want from life by believing that you have already got it. You have become temporarily insane. It is wonderful to be in a loving relationship, but it needn't rob you of your individuality. Remember, he/she fell in love with the person you once were, not the robotic, emotional, dependent neurotic you seem to have become.

What happens when you are "in love?"

- Your conscious mind becomes totally absorbed by the new "love in your life," and you lose sight of everything else

- Your conscious mind is filled with thoughts that occupy you and can control you
- On a subconscious level you have things you want to achieve, but when your conscious mind believes you are happy, it blocks out all other thoughts.

Be honest with yourself. Identify where you are losing your power. In your mind, take yourself through the pattern of your behavior that allows loss of power. What small thing can you change in order to retain some small element of power?

Attainable Goals

Remember, it is important to only allow yourself to take one small step at a time. The first small step is "don't react." Stay focused on the outcome you want to achieve. Don't spread yourself too thinly. Taking small steps allows you time to focus. Take time for yourself to understand the process and time to re-energize. You will be able to focus your energy on one target. The process will be slow, but stay in the moment and be dedicated to learning this new behavior. It will give you rewards. Persistence and patience are the keys to achieving your short-term goals, targets and eventual success. Remember, it is rare for you to achieve total success on your first try.

Measurable Goals

Learn to measure the small changes you make to your lifestyle and behavior. You can do this, easily, by taking stock of the circumstances, reviewing the situation and identifying how things have changed.

- What did you do to change the particular issue?
- What was the outcome of the change in pattern?
- Did it benefit you?
- Was it more calm?
- Did the situation resolve itself more easily?

These answers will clearly indicate the measure of your success so far.

What should your strategy contain?

Your strategy should contain some simple statements that will be the foundation of your new belief system, geared to create and maintain your relationship after forgiveness has taken place.

Here are some examples:

- Decide to take some time out of your day to clear the clutter of grudges from your mind
- Deciding to forgive someone is to make a decision
- Decide to forgive today
- Practice forgiving the small stuff. Move on to the heavy stuff when you are comfortable to do so
- Challenge your negative thoughts and make a decision to change them to positive thoughts
- Acknowledge that it is unreasonable to expect your partner or other people to be respectful and decent all of the time. Remember to err is human
- Accept that mistakes often occur, so don't take mistakes personally. If you find that you do take a mistake personally, address it immediately and move on.

To forgive your partner or someone else enables you to move on in your own life. The act of forgiveness breaks the chain of resentment and hurt that has imprisoned and tied you to your perceived enemy for too long. You are the one who will benefit from breaking the chain. You will experience the freedom when bitterness, hurt and resentment are finally released and dissolved. Hurt, pain, hostility, resentment, bitterness, and hatred are all poisoned emotions that you hold within you. You are the only one hurt by this poison. Your perceived enemy is carrying on in their life, sometimes completely unaware that you are holding all these negative emotions against them. Making a conscious decision to let go of all these destructive emotions cleanses your mind, body and soul.

When you have made the decision to forgive someone, the first hurdle has already been jumped. Forgiving someone is an act of compassion that tells the person you are forgiving that you are prepared to put the past behind you and will harbor no grudges against them. In doing this, let me make it clear that you are not condoning what the person said or did, nor are you giving that person permission to do the same thing to you again. Forgiving someone does not give them *carte blanche* to treat you badly.

There is a big gap between forgiving and forgetting but if you truly forgive, I believe that it is possible to walk from forgiving to forgetting as time passes by. If you are able to eventually forget also, then this will enable both you and your partner to begin rebuilding and re-establishing your relationship.

4	# What Is Blame?

"To say or think that someone or something did something wrong or is responsible for something bad happening."

Blaming may often involve diverting responsibility from oneself. You can't play the "blame" game alone. It requires at least two people—the partner who blames, and the receiver of the blame. The protagonist (this is the partner projecting the blame) places the blame on to the receiver (partner) for something that has been said or done. The receiver of the blame is the partner who will be made to feel guilty.

Blame and Guilt, in this context, are emotional tools that are projected on to another person to make them feel bad and accept full responsibility and accountability for the misdeed. Blame and Guilt are repeated negative patterns that are firmly established in your belief system. It is only when things go wrong in a relationship that this repeated negative pattern is challenged. It will never be challenged if the receiver of the blame continually accepts that he/she is responsible for the misdeed.

Blame and Guilt are not healthy emotions. They are both destructive emotional weapons used in the worst possible way to manipulate and render the receiver powerless. Blame and Guilt will only work if the receiver is prepared to accept them. If the receiver is not prepared to accept the blame and guilt and does not accept responsibility and accountability for the misdeed, then the protagonist (the blamer) is beaten and will lose the "game." It only takes one partner to drop the ball in the "blame" game and the problem will be solved.

How does being "blamed" feel when on the receiving end?

Here are some examples:

If you accept blame...

- You will feel disempowered and emotionally disabled
- You are giving in and surrendering to your partner (the protagonist)
- When you know you haven't done anything, then you are colluding with your partner and will stay locked in the "game"
- You will feel persecuted
- You will feel worthless
- You are doing yourself a disservice
- You should ask yourself, "Why am I continuing to do this—what's in it for me?"
- You are in a negative controlling situation.

Why is blame passed to someone else?

Here are some examples:

Blame is passed to someone else for the blamer...

- To avoid taking responsibility and accountability
- To reinforce the "victim" stance of the receiver
- To delay making decisions
- To appear innocent.

There are many reasons why blame is passed on. I am sure you can add to this list.

What is a victim?

"A victim is someone who suffers through no fault of his/her own." A victim places the control of their behavior and their life on to someone else. They project to others that they are innocent victims and are powerless in controlling their own lives. We're not talking about a victim of a crime here, such as being robbed at gunpoint. No, this type of "victim" is much more insidious, we're talking about victimhood as a lifestyle choice.

Here are some examples of what a "victim" believes or does:

- Victims believe that life is something that happens to them which they have no control over
- Victims believe that they are innocent
- Victims feel trapped
- Victims believe that people/situations block their path from having what they want
- Victims control other people (their partner) by blaming them for their unhappy state, thereby absolving themselves of responsibility
- Victims believe that they can do nothing right
- Victims focus on injustices that they believe others are directing at them
- Victims identify the weakness their partner exhibits and manipulate their targets into accepting blame in order to gain power and control
- Victims suffer stress, anxiety and depression
- Victims are obsessive in holding on to hurt and pain
- Victims are *takers* and will rob other people of energy and enthusiasm (they are blood sucking parasites).

Here are some examples of negative responses to being victimized:

- To be at someone's mercy
- To smile when you want to cry
- To pretend that everything is alright
- To tip-toe around someone all the time (treading on egg shells)
- To do their bidding, no matter the consequences to yourself

- To give up on yourself
- To become nondescript
- To have a low self-esteem
- To block out your emotions
- To be unloved
- To flatline.

Here are some positive responses on how to deal with victimization:

- Don't be afraid to show your feelings, learn when it is appropriate to do this
- Encourage open discussions to enable you both to have a better understanding of each other
- Realize you are never going to get it right, so stop trying
- Be reasonable, flexible and fair in your responses, but know when enough is enough (you will know when this happens by the feeling in your gut)
- Treat yourself kindly
- Realize how much you have achieved
- Don't be afraid to recognize your needs, wants and desires—you have a right to them
- Accept that you "can't have it all" but make sure you "get some"
- Take charge of yourself and know that any change you want to achieve in your life is up to you.

Victims (blamers) usually become this way through their early childhood experiences. If a child is repeatedly told by a parent that they are bad, this can result in the child establishing a pattern of behavior which is rooted in guilt and blame. The child will believe that there are aspects of themselves that are really bad (even when this is not true), and so the pattern is guaranteed to continue into adulthood. It is when the blamer enters into an intimate relationship with someone that the pattern from childhood is revealed.

Relationships are two-sided in that your partner will see the very best of you and will also see the very worst of you. Because most people are unaware of repeating emotional negative patterns derived from their childhood, they don't know what to look out for during arguments or even during general interactions with their partner. Most people believe "what you see is what you get." People, generally, are unaware of "hidden agendas" and "patterns of behavior." A child doesn't learn in school about the many different types of communication, where they come from and how to change it if it continually gets you into a difficult situation. It is only in adult life after having the experience of feeling miserable, let down, disabled, and emotionally spent, do we start looking at why this is happening to us.

How do you rid yourself of an established pattern that is getting difficult to manage?

Here is what you can do to change the situation:

- Acknowledge that you are following a pattern. You can do this by looking closely at the words and behavior you use during arguments with your partner
- See that you are a key player in the interaction between you and your partner
- Accept that you can do very little to change anyone else
- Take responsibility for your part in the argument
- Ask yourself, "What do I gain by behaving in this way in blaming my partner?"
- Decide to stop blaming your partner
- Decide to release your pattern of behavior that causes you to blame your partner
- Be honest and open when you communicate with your partner

- Decide to rid yourself of "secrets" from the past that are the cause of making you feel guilty and therefore a victim
- Take a good look at your friends and family and ask yourself, "Do these people inspire and empower me or are they actually assisting me to stay the way I am— disempowered?"
- Seek the companionship of assertive, enthusiastic, independent, empowering people and emulate them
- Take risks and feel free of the burdens you have been carrying
- Get support from trusted family and friends while you are releasing your patterns of behavior that are no longer useful to you.

Letting go of blame:

This is an exercise I would like you to try in order to clearly see the effect that blaming your partner has on you:

1. Write down an argument that you have had with your partner, which you find difficult to forgive and forget.
2. Next, think of how much energy you have used in continuing thinking of this particular argument.
3. Ask yourself, "How do I feel when I think of this argument?"
4. Ask yourself, "What is my role in this argument?"
5. Are you aware that you are behaving like a victim?
6. Are you aware that you are behaving like a martyr?
7. Are you aware that you are opting out of taking responsibility?
8. Are you aware that you are the perpetrator of placing the blame onto your partner?
9. Ask yourself, "Am I hooked into the belief that I will not be liked by my partner if I am the guilty one?"

10. Ask yourself, "How does this thought make me feel about myself?'

11. Ask yourself, "Why do I feel the need to absolve myself of any wrongdoing?"

12. Ask yourself, "Do I want to release these negative beliefs about myself in order to become an emotionally independent person?"

Now, let's go back to the argument you identified at the beginning of this exercise. Do you still feel hurt and pain? Do you still believe that you are blameless? Are you still absolving yourself of any blame? Are you able to see that you had your role to play in the argument? Can you identify your role in the argument?

If you can answer these questions in a positive way, you are in the process of "moving on" from your old belief system that resulted in you blaming others.

This is a useful exercise you can apply to all the arguments and disagreements that are destroying your relationship with your partner, and with other people you hold accountable for deeds you believe have been targeted at you. If you are able to apply this exercise to all the areas in which you are unable to forgive, you will see that you will be able to rid yourself of them successfully.

> "Every saint has a past and every sinner has a future."
>
> Oscar Wilde

5 | **Defusing Conflict and Communication**

The truth about communicating with your partner:

- There is only one person who can make you happy—YOU.
- There is only one person who can give you unconditional love—YOU (discounting God or your pet).
- There is only one person you can change—YOU.
- You can be with your partner and still feel lonely.
- Effective communication begins by listening to your partner.
- You only really grow in your relationship through experiences and overcoming difficulties.
- Your marriage begins when your fantasy is crushed.

Men in Communication and Conflict

We'll start our analysis of communication and conflict with the male side. While I can't of course describe every man in a couple of paragraphs, bear with me while we examine a typical sort of male. I believe that most men are ego-led. This means that they are fragile and sensitive to any form of criticism. A man is wary of opening up and being honest with a partner, fearing that he will be laughed at, ridiculed and embarrassed. Men need a lot of ego stroking and constant acknowledgement of all the things that they do for you. Most men are good at expressing their opinion on any given subject, but less likely to listen to and acknowledge yours.

- A man doesn't want to be judged by you, but will judge you. He believes it is his right
- A man expects to control and be in charge of a relationship, although he will be adamant in his portrayal that he believes he has an equal partnership with you
- If you dare challenge a man, he will retreat to his cave in response
- A man doesn't expect to change his habits or beliefs in a relationship, but will believe he has a right to expect you to change
- A man will ask for your opinion, but will believe it to be reasonable to proceed his way
- Men like being in control of financial arrangements
- If you want to have a successful relationship with your man, this can only be achieved by reducing your expectations of him.

An equal partnership requires mutual openness between the two of you. In my experience, men are less inclined to reveal all their past relationships to their partners. Women on the other hand are prepared to reveal all. Men are good at remembering the things you have told them about yourself early on in your relationship, and will use this information against you if necessary in order to stay in control and be top dog. When a man explains something to you, he will not want to hear your views. He will reject your comments if you point out something that you think he has done wrong. He wants you to agree with him on all levels and will believe you are unreasonable if you cannot do this. When you are out with friends and a difference of opinion is exposed and discussed, your man will expect you to side with him at any cost to your beliefs. Don't try and teach him anything—he already knows it. There are many types of different music, but a man can only dance to one tune, his own.

To be able to "move on" in your relationship with your man, it is important to understand that you cannot remind him of something he said last year or even yesterday, because he won't remember it unless it is to his advantage to do so. The very act of remembering something he said or did in the past will result in him withdrawing from you and not trusting you in the future. In entering a relationship with your man, it is advantageous to understand and accept the way he perceives his role and responsibility in the relationship. Be sure not to get the roles and responsibilities wrong, because getting him to change his ways is a very difficult task to undertake. In order to have a satisfactory relationship with your man, you are the one who will have to listen carefully in order to hear his non-verbal communication to you, and furthermore he will expect you to anticipate his thoughts and reactions to most things that he says. He, however, will not think twice about the non-verbal communication you are giving him. Understand here and now that your man is not going to be totally honest in his relationship with you. Very few people are, because they are scared of the reaction that follows total honesty. When you begin to discover the real man in your life, you will be faced with some searching questions to ask yourself:

- Do you like him?
- Can you tolerate his behavior and beliefs?
- Are you afraid of his reactions?
- Do you want to know the ins and outs of his past?
- Can you face the reality of knowing who and what he is?
- Have you been brave and challenged him?
- Do you want to continue in the relationship?

If you have answered positively to these questions, are you the woman of his dreams?

Women in Communication and Conflict

I hope you didn't think that I was not going to examine the female stance in communicating in relationships. Again, while no stereotype is perfect, we can speak in some general terms.

- Women analyze every facial twitch, nuance and reaction of her man
- Women are ready to point out how to make things better
- Women can behave like "victims" and martyrs in the space of 5 minutes
- Women are manipulators
- Women acquire power in their relationship by devious methods
- Women don't always say what they think
- A woman will absorb any gossip she hears about her man's past
- Women will search through coats and jackets in their quest to know all
- Women are cleverer than men
- Women are more aware of the feelings of other people
- Women are good friends, but spiteful enemies
- Women harbor a grudge longer than men do
- Women like powerful men
- Women want their man to protect them
- Women are chameleons
- Women respond to charm, love and affection
- Women are more aware than men.

Being in a relationship with a woman is comparatively easy. She wants shows of affection. She wants her man to be strong emotionally and physically. She wants her man to listen and hear what she says. She wants to be included in decision-making. She wants to have her own way some of the time. She does not want to be taken for granted. She does not want her man to mistake her for his mother. She wants her man to do his fair share around the home. She wants equality with regard to joint finances.

Women enjoy nurturing and giving unconditional love. Men love receiving it. Women are aware of their conflicting emotions and feelings. Men are not. Nor do they make excuses for themselves. In order to have a successful relationship with your woman, she will need to believe that her man is honest, reliable, dependable, loving, fair, non-judgmental, happy-go-lucky, financially secure, flexible and adaptable, and not addicted to the television with particular reference to sport of any sort. Are you this man?

A woman is expected to forgive and forget a lot of things regarding the man in her life. Fortunately, most emotionally intelligent women can do this. Women are more adaptable and flexible than most men, and as a result are able to take on board the necessary changes to be made.

It may seem that I am being too picky and overzealous in my observations regarding men and women. I believe that the more knowledge is available to you, the better equipped you are in living with and loving each other. Forgiving each other the idiosyncrasies that are inherent in each of us will be crucial in order to have a healthy loving relationship. Constant forgiveness guarantees constant love.

A healthy loving relationship that is constantly growing is impossible to achieve without forgiveness. It is impossible to have a loving relationship with someone if you are holding on to stuff that has happened to you in your past, or even in your current relationship. If something has happened in your present relationship that you are experiencing difficulty in overcoming, you must let it go if you want the relationship to continue.

You must understand that in order to love someone else/your partner, you must learn to love yourself first. None of us are taught how to love ourselves. In fact, we are taught to put other people's needs before our own. I believe this to be a mistake. I believe that if you are all right with yourself, you are better placed to love, support and help others. Some people find it difficult to move on from past hurts, and by not moving on what they are actively doing is investing their energy into long forgotten misdeeds that they are still hanging onto.

Forgiving people from your past is an essential element in living a healthy emotional life now. If you are unable to forgive people from your past, you will be unable to form a healthy relationship in the here and now, because your emotional belief system has not moved on and is still linked to that person and unhealthy hurt and pain. Acknowledge the struggle you are experiencing in hanging on to old hurts. Acknowledge the struggle you are experiencing in your relationship now and ask yourself, "Why am I struggling?"

> "The things that two people in love do to each other they remember. And if they stay together, it is not because they forget, it is because they forgive."
> *Indecent Proposal* (1993) with Robert Redford and Demi Moore

To forgive someone is to free yourself from the prison of your past. Forgiving someone takes courage, but it does not mean that you will forget the incident. It does mean, however, that you have accepted, forgiven and moved on from the bad memories you have clung to. When, in the future, you remember the incident (and you will), you must also remind yourself that you have chosen to forgive. The past is just that—the past. You are here now, so it is the present and the future that should concern you. Forgiveness enables you to cut ties with resentment, bitterness, hatred, obsession, anger, and pain. Forgiveness does not necessarily mean that you have to reconcile and talk with someone who has treated you badly, but it is the key to your future happiness.

Forgiveness made easy

- It is easier to forgive someone who apologizes to you for their part in the problem
- It is easier to forgive someone if this person tries to change the way they interact with you
- It is easier to forgive someone who wants to resume contact with you.

If you decide not to forgive someone, you are choosing to stay in the role of "victim." Think about it like this. If you do not forgive someone and stay in the role of "victim," you are surrendering your energy, power and control to the person you will not forgive. You are sabotaging yourself, your relationship and your future, because you are inexorably linking to the memory and to the person you cannot forgive. Remember that the best sort of revenge is success. You will not be successful if you hang on to past unhappy and hurtful circumstances. Reliving this experience gives the person you are unable to forgive power over you. Focus your thinking on healing and moving on rather than being stuck in your emotional development.

> "Always forgive your enemies—nothing annoys them so much."
>
> Oscar Wilde

Getting unstuck and communicating

We hear the words "move on" all the time. But the essential question to ask is "How do you do that?" The words are easy to say but difficult to put into context and also difficult to achieve. I have already established in this book that if you are unforgiving of your partner, then you are holding on to a negative attachment with that person. This attachment not only affects the value you put on yourself; if affects several of your other needs.

Here are some examples of what I mean:

- It affects the way you perceive yourself
- It affects your sense of fair play
- It affects your sense of justification
- It affects your basic belief system
- It affects your confidence, self-worth and values.

You will be unable to "move on" until you understand and find answers to these points. That will allow you to self-heal.

Again, it is easy to say the words, "don't hold on to negativity," but exactly how do you do this?

You cannot hold negativity in your hand.

You cannot see negativity sitting on a shelf.

Negativity is inside you and you feel it like a big black bomb in the pit of your stomach. The answer to the question, "How do you rid yourself of negativity?" is to "decide to do it." Decide that you no longer want this feeling or the burden festering in the pit of your stomach.

Here is an exercise to help you rid yourself of hurt and pain:

1. Write down the name/s of the person/s you need to forgive.
2. Next, write each of them a letter clearly outlining the hurt and pain they have caused you, and how this hurt and pain has affected your life.
3. Next, make a firm decision to forgive this person/s.
4. Next, write a second letter to each of these people informing them that you have decided to forgive them.
5. Next, put the letters away in a safe place.

This exercise on its own will not rid you of the negative thoughts, but it will give you a structure to focus on during the times you feel particularly angry toward this person/s. During these times, re-read the letters you have written, and this action will re-confirm the decision you have made to yourself to forgive. In my experience in order to "move on" from hurt and pain, you need to put the thought of hurt, pain and forgiveness into action, i.e., the writing of the letters. It is far easier to overcome hurt and pain if you have a tangible, practical routine to help you. Accept that you will struggle with your decision to forgive this person/s. Your own ego will try its best to stop you doing this by further justifying the negative thoughts you have experienced in wanting revenge. Continuing with this exercise will help you in the healing process of forgiving, and you will begin to notice your anger and hostility ebb away, and in its place will be acceptance and forgiveness. The final ceremony of this exercise is reading each letter for the last time and burning it. As the letter burns, so your resentment and hostility will recede, and your understanding and forgiveness will come to the forefront of your mind.

A vital and important aspect of forgiving and forgetting is the value you place on your relationship. If your relationship is healthy, you will value your relationship with your partner more than you care about being right in the argument. Even on the occasions that you know you are definitely having all the facts on your side, you should acknowledge that being right should not be at the expense of ruining your relationship. If you are able to put your love for your partner before the fact that you are right, you will be more able and willing to forgive and forget and move on. Sometimes your partner will be right and sometimes you will be right. Who cares? Why don't you both regard the disagreement as a good discussion where you both accept having opposite opinions? If you can do this, you will be actively working through the difficulty and conflict, and this will make your relationship stronger as a result of this action.

Here is an example of a structure you can use to discuss your disagreements and difficulties:

- Jointly agree on a time to discuss the issue
- Do not have the discussion until your emotions have settled down and you are able to be calm and logical

- Try to find a mutually satisfactory answer rather than concentrating on being right
- During the discussion do not resort to throwing up past problems and guilts
- If there is more than one issue to address, engage in each one separately. Do not confuse the issue by going back and forward on each
- Make sure that both of you give each other ample time to give an opinion on the issue.
- Concentrate on what your partner is talking out, rather than rehearsing an answer aimed at sabotaging the discussion
- Always look at the bigger picture, not just your take on it. This is the way forward to avoid being subjective and selfish and always wanting to be right
- Remember that your love for one another is the primary concern, and sometimes being in love with your partner means letting him/her be right even when you know for certain that they are not
- Be forgiving of misdemeanors.

"He who covers over an offense promotes love, but whoever repeats the matter separates close friends."

Proverbs 17:9, *KJV*

| 6 | **Overcoming Obstacles** |

What are obstacles?

"An obstacle is a hindrance and an obstruction."

It is important for you to live together in harmony. Life outside your relationship is difficult enough without having to cope with constant conflicts within your intimate relationship with your partner. In order to live in a safe haven, you have to set about creating one. You can create a peaceful environment if you both feel you would benefit from doing this. Let's face it, who wouldn't benefit from a safe, loving environment?

Overcoming Obstacles

What are the obstacles that you need to overcome?

To help you identify what your particular obstacles are, try this exercise:

1. Talk with your partner to identify exactly what obstacles are causing a barrier between you. Write them down.
2. Talk with your partner in order to identify why you cannot cross this barrier, and write it down.
3. Tell each other about three grudges you are holding on to with regard to your relationship, and write them down.
4. Name three unrealistic expectations you have subscribed to in your relationship, and write them down.

When you have done these things, discuss each obstacle, grudge and unrealistic expectation that you have subscribed to in your relationship, and find ways to erase or limit them. If you are harboring grudges against your partner, make a decision to let them go so that you can both move on in your relationship. Instead of harboring grudges, focus on the positive qualities of your partner. Remember that engaging with your partner in this way will draw you closer together. Honesty is essential in this exercise.

Here is another useful example of an exercise you can do together in order to overcome obstacles:

You both should identify the problem you are most concerned with.

1. Ask yourselves, "Does this problem only exist in our home, or elsewhere also?"

2. Name and write down the person you are having the problem with.

3. Ask yourself and each other, "Is this person important to me/us?"

4. Ask yourself and each other, "Does this person know that I/we are finding being around him/her difficult?"

5. Ask yourself and each other, "If I was able to talk to this person and tell him/her how I feel, would he/she be able to work through this problem with me?" If the answer to this question is no, you will have to stop here. Don't bother digging deep and uncovering why this person is unable to work through the conflict with you. Accept and move on should this happen. If the answer is "yes," you are able to proceed with the exercise.

6. How should my behavior change in order to resolve the problem?

7. Are we both operating from the same belief system?

Take as much time as you need with this exercise. It is complicated, and in order to get the best results you should both be clear in your answers. When you believe that you have answered the questions and both agree with the answers, you can put a plan together in order to address the problem.

Here is an example of an action plan:

- We now realize that our problem is...
- We now realize after much discussion that the solution(s) to it is...
- We have both decided to treat each other with respect and sensitivity
- If necessary, we will seek professional help for our problems
- We fully intend to handle slip-ups and setbacks by...
- We will jointly review this plan regularly
- If we both deem it necessary, we will re-create this action plan
- We will both know if this plan is successful when we resolve our present conflict
- We are both prepared to sign up and commit to the action plan.

Don't give in and give up

During this stage of your relationship, it might seem easier to give in and give up. If, however, you both face the challenge of repairing and recreating your relationship, you will be seen by your partner as being dedicated and determined to overcome these conflicts, so that you can both move on to a successful long-term relationship. When a relationship is neglected it is like a potted plant that has not been watered for a very long time. The plant will droop and be pot bound, weeds will spring up and the earth will be arid. The plant will require gentle nurturing to become healthy again. The same principle applies to your relationship. With grit and determination you will pass through this rough time and you will be re-planting a new relationship based on trust, honesty, open communication and loyalty.

You will encounter many obstacles on your journey through your life. Part of living and learning is finding out how to deal with obstacles and how to overcome them. You can do this by using the "4 point tool:"

- Do not expect your relationship with your partner to be perfect
- Learn to love your partner despite his/her faults
- Aim for honest communication with your partner
- Do not expect your partner to metamorphose into the fantasy partner of your dreams. This is an unrealistic expectation. Remember that your dream state is a fantasy, not reality.

Along the road to achieving a healthy relationship, you will be uncovering myths that you have both believed in.

Let's take a look at myths:

Myths

What is a myth?

"An imaginary person or thing or fictitious story or legend."

Wouldn't it be great if your imaginary person or imaginary life were to become a reality? The bad news is this is not going to happen. The good news is you will have a lot of worthwhile, life enhancing experiences in your journey to creating the life you want. What are the myths in relationships?

This is my list of myths:

- Myth #1: The euphoric feeling when you first fall in love will last forever.
- Myth #2: You will feel "in love" all the time.
- Myth #3: There is something wrong with your relationship because you don't enjoy the same things.

- Myth #4: Expecting your partner to be responsible for your happiness.
- Myth #5: You will know immediately when you have found "the one."
- Myth #6: When you are in a committed relationship you will have sex every night.
- Myth #7: Your partner should just understand you without you having to communicate with him or her.
- Myth #8: Living together will prepare you for marriage and improve your chances of being happily married.
- Myth #9: If my partner would just change, my relationship would be great.
- Myth #10: I have to say what I feel.
- Myth #11: The perfect partner would make my life complete.
- Myth #12: If my partner was honest, I could accept anything he/she did.

These are the myths that are significant for me. You can add to this list.

Conflicting During Communication

In order to successfully overcome obstacles, it is relevant to take a look at the type of communication between yourself and your partner during conflicts.

Wanting to win at all costs

If you or your partner behaves in an authoritative and/or domineering manner, this behavior identifies that the person puts his/her needs before his/her partner. This person operates from the standpoint of, "I win you lose."

The aggressive (bully) person

The person displaying a bullying attitude (physical or mental) will manipulate his/her partner in order to get power and control over him/her.

The aggressive (charmer) person

This form of aggression is done by lying and persuasion, and this type of person uses these skills to persuade his/her partner to do what the charmer wants. He/she is a professional salesperson in achieving his/her aim.

The aggressive (judgmental) person

This form of aggression is used to keep one's partner feeling guilty and responsible for what he/she has or hasn't done. This type of aggressive personality is always right and always expects to have power over their partner. The person who partners with a judgmental person will believe that they are not as clever as their partner and will bend to his/her will.

The aggressive (being nice) person

This behavior is a gentler form of getting your own way. It is a very powerful way of interacting with your partner, as it is displayed by "giving up" control to the "nice person." This is the behavior of a "victim" who wants to opt out of responsibility. The relationship between partners will work if one partner is a "victim" and the other partner is a "martyr."

The aggressive (I am the boss) person

This is the historical method of marriage and partnerships when women were perceived as the weaker sex, and men were the breadwinners. Women who are attracted to strong powerful men give in to "the stronger partner," easily believing that this is the right thing to do. This belief system usually comes about as a result of observing and copying early role models. A man who uses this method of interacting with his partner will have his strength, power and ego reinforced, and will create an unequal partnership which secures his place in the relationship (she can't do without me).

The aggressive partner meets his/her aggressive counterpart

When an aggressive partner marries an aggressive partner, stand back and watch the sparks fly. There will be a considerable amount of unsolvable conflict between these two people as both vie to control the other. Such people are usually distrustful in intimate relationships, and until one or both surrender their control they will live with "locked horns" and will be unable to develop together and move on.

The single factor permeating all of the above styles of engaging in a relationship is "control." It's getting what one partner wants from their partner, who allows it to continue.

A healthy communicative relationship should be "win-win." This equal status will reinforce that both partners have equal power, trust, love, energy, and security.

It is disappointing when you come to the conclusion that your partner doesn't meet your needs. This very thought suggests that you are expecting your partner to be all the things you want him/her to be to make you happy. Often, you will not find out your partner's imperfections until you have been together for some time. When conflict arises and you become upset, the person who feels disappointed will blame this on their partner, which reinforces their disappointment in that person. This reaction confirms that the disappointed partner is putting their happiness and wellbeing on their partner's shoulders.

To some extent you (the disappointed person) are creating your own unhappiness by placing too much responsibility on your partner.

- Everyone has a basic right to be who they really are
- Everyone has a basic right to expect their partner to have an equal voice and equal input into the relationship
- Everyone has a right to expect that their partner will take equal responsibility for the relationship.

When none of these expectations are present, it will be a difficult relationship to maintain and a disaster waiting to happen.

Suggestions for what should exist in your relationship:
- Forgiveness is an essential element in healthy relationships
- Honesty is an essential element in healthy relationships
- Communication is an essential element in healthy relationships
- Trust is an essential element in healthy relationships
- Security is an essential element in healthy relationships.

The biggest issue women, particularly, have is caused by their desire to mend or change their partner. These women believe that they cannot love their partner unless that person changes their behavior. The other partner is left feeling hurt and inferior, as though something is wrong with them. The phrase that springs to mind is, "If you loved me as you say you do, you would do as I ask and change your ways." Unfortunately that saying is not based on reality. True love is allowing your partner to be as they are, accepting them as they are, and continuing to love them despite your differences. Ask yourself, "Why did I set up home with my partner in the first place?" You each should take responsibility for creating a loving relationship. Living life is about learning, growing and developing, and celebrating becoming a balanced individual.

Basically, it is necessary to realize that as you are, right now at this moment, is where you are meant to be, so that you can experience conflict, trust, responsibility, love, and experience differences in each other. If you see your life as an adventure and conflict as a hurdle to overcome and move on, your differences might be easier to accept and move along with.

"Bear with each another and forgive whatever grievances you may have against one another. Forgive as the Lord forgave you."

Colossians 3:13, *KJV*

7	**Designing Your Action Plan**

In order to live the life you want after you have forgiven someone/your partner, you have to reinvent it. You can do this. You can transform your life:

- By changing yourself you can be who you want to be
- Changing yourself will alter your outlook on yourself and your partner
- Changing yourself will make all things possible.

The mind has two major parts: the conscious and the unconscious. The conscious mind is the bit we use to think through a problem. The unconscious is where our feelings, beliefs and memories live, and this part of our brain does not use logic—it "thinks" symbolically.

In order to make positive changes in past negative patterns, you cannot see yourself as powerless. This thought will totally disable you. If you see yourself as powerless, you are denying yourself the enjoyment of the reaching for and experiencing the power that is rightfully yours.

If you think you don't have power in the situation you are in, try this exercise:

- What would be three ways in which you could make your situation worse?
- If you have found three ways to make your situation worse, then can you also find three ways in which you can make it better?

In order to empower yourself, you need to understand that your thinking and beliefs have to be clear and positive. Effort and struggle are all signs that you are fighting with yourself—that you are at cross purposes with your own deeply held belief system.

Your mind is the control center of your behavior, and your behavior is what determines how you are perceived and what you accomplish in life.

The first thing to do if you decide you want to change your negative pattern of behavior is to take responsibility for where you are now. Don't blame yourself for everything that's gone wrong in your life. Indulging in this thought process can only lead to feelings of regret and "if only." These thoughts will leave you feeling negative and lacking in energy. You need your batteries charged and filled with energy to change yourself.

Remember that you will only become disappointed if you have expectations of others.

- Are you always ready to blame someone else for not making you happy?
- Are you always ready to blame your partner for not giving you the love you want?
- Are you always ready to blame your partner for not providing you with a comfortable existence?
- Ask yourself, "Am I placing the responsibility for my happiness and future comforts on someone else?"
- Ask yourself, "Am I putting another person/my partner under considerable pressure (albeit unintentionally) to give me what I want?"
- Ask yourself "Why do I do this?"

The answer to this last question is, "You do it because you do not believe you can do all these things for yourself." You have no self worth or self confidence. You have no faith in your ability to give yourself what you want, so you opt out and try to get these things through someone else's abilities. You should think for yourself and not put the responsibility for your happiness on another person.

Most people spend the majority of their lives reacting to situations and people.

You do this because:

- You believe you have the right to speak up for yourself
- You believe you have the right to an opinion
- You believe you have a right to answer back when confronted with an issue
- You believe you are a person in your own right and you value yourself.

You have probably lived by these principles throughout your life within personal relationships with the opposite sex. Ask yourself, "Does this belief system work in my current relationship?" Has your relationship failed because you have stuck to your belief system?

Accept the following:

- You don't have to always say what you feel
- You don't always have to stand up and be counted
- You don't always have to solve other people's problems and issues for them
- You don't always have to offer an opinion.

Accept that you always have a choice in how to react in a situation. The single most powerful lesson you will learn is to be still in the mind and shut up.

I believe that most women are "people pleasers." What this means is that women are like chameleons, changing to suit whoever they are with at any given time. I believe that women who are in love do this automatically without even recognizing what they are doing. Women make excuses for themselves and their actions. Women make excuses for their partners.

Women have the ability to see things clearly from the other person's point of view, and are better able to adapt their behavior in order to accommodate their partner and make them happy at any cost to themselves so that the relationship stays the same. Women surrender control of the relationship to their partner without realizing what they are actually doing and the effect this will have on their mental health in the long term.

In order to move on after forgiving your partner, you should follow your action plan and consider your options regarding not *reacting* to every situation, sentence, nuance and facial expression your partner uses. This task is challenging if you are a reactive person. You must be determined, however, to try your best and see what happens.

Here are two examples on staying focused on your decision and how to deliberately stop yourself answering questions:

- Divert the conversation
- Leave the room on some pretence, to allow you some time to think of an appropriate response or, indeed, to decide not to respond at all.

You will be amazed at the difference in the dynamics of the relationship when you engage in this method of resisting conflict. Peace reigns for quite some considerable time. When asked a question by your partner, you could pretend you don't know the answer and wait until your partner arrives at their own conclusions. At first waiting for a situation to change is frustrating, but if you stick to it you will enjoy the feeling of not being pressured to have the answers and find solutions.

There are little tricks you can adopt along the way in changing your responses. For instance, if you are asked a question you don't want to answer, look directly at a third party; when you do this the focus of the person asking the question will transfer from you on to the third party, and it is this person who will be expected to answer the question. If you don't know the answer/or the answer you want to give is too contentious, look at someone else and they automatically take the responsibility for answering the question. Try it. Try to keep this non-reaction up—that's all you do at this time. Do nothing else. I think is is a mistake when trying to change negative patterns within yourself is to do too much too soon. Just do that one simple task and continue doing it for a few months. Don't be tempted to bring anything else into the equation. Lie fallow. Rest your mind during this time, and watch others around you change the way they handle situations without you being involved in the decision process. This simple adjustment has many benefits.

Here are some examples:
- You can't be blamed if things go wrong
- You maintain your energy
- You become an observer rather than a participant
- You are not responsible for the outcome
- You are not seen as a "know-it-all"
- You will observe that your partner/others will be forced to think and solve problems without your intervention
- You allow others to grow up
- You allow others to take responsibility for their behavior, speech, and actions
- You observe the development of ideas and thoughts around you
- You see you are not needed to solve everything
- You are not the "bad guy" anymore

These are just a few of the points you will observe while in this stage of your action plan.

Always stay in the here and now. When situations arise that you can feel are spiraling out of control, stay in reality.

See it for what it is. Remember other situations that were similar and stick with it.

- Remember other situations and ask yourself, "Where did they lead on to?"
- Remember and ask, "What exactly happened?"
- Remember and ask, "What was the outcome?'

If you have done this, ask yourself, "Is there any need to be frightened or driven to sort things out and please my partner at my own expense? Is there any need to avoid disastrous outcomes and consequences?"

Remember that it is important that you stay in control of your emotions. Don't let your partner override your stance by bullying you, intimidating you or interrogating you. *Stay in reality.* Think about what your partner actually wants from the process they are engaging you in. If you think carefully and objectively, you will know the underlying problem and the anticipated outcome. Take stock. Don't panic. Think. Above all else—*don't react.*

Staying focused and realistic when faced with an emotional problem is the hardest thing to do, because of course you are involved.

- Take yourself outside the problem
- Look at the characters involved
- What did your partner expect the outcome to be?
- Realistically, what can you do to make it better?

If you stay realistic and keep a clear head and a still tongue, the situation will resolve itself. When you are in a difficult situation, it is natural to want to make it better. You must accept that the responsibility is not yours alone.

Being realistic has its benefits, for example:

- You stay in the here and now
- You give yourself time to unravel your fears, thoughts and actions
- You allow others to think things through on their own

- You allow time for people to come to their own conclusions
- You don't react in a panic
- You have the time to find out what it is you want to achieve
- You find out the outcome the others want to achieve
- You reassess your principles, values and beliefs
- You let the dust settle
- You give yourself time to just be
- You live in the moment of each day.

To some extent all of us live in a fantasy world of our own making. All of us want to live a fairy tale life. All of us want happiness, health and an uncomplicated life. All of us want to be loved and adored.

- Reality is knowing where you have come from, where you are now and where you want to go.
- Reality is setting short term goals in place in order to achieve at least some of your desires.
- Reality is to understand the person you are dealing with, where they have come from, where they are now and where they want to go.

It's about knowing the people you love and finding the best realistic option in dealing with every situation that presents itself.

Staying focused means getting those distractions out of the way that are keeping you from accomplishing what you want. Life is full of ways to become distracted. Decide to become self-disciplined. If you stay focused, eventually things will slot into place, and peace will reign once more.

These are some tips for staying focused:

- Keep your reason for staying focused in the forefront of your mind
- Remember the saying, "The road to hell is paved with good intentions." You can have all the best intentions

in the world, but if you don't see them through they are worthless

- Be motivated. Stay firm. Discipline yourself
- Switch your mind from the negative thought you are focused on to something positive you want to happen
- Don't listen to anyone else's advice. Nothing must put you off
- Don't let your family and friends run over you
- Allow some time for yourself each day. Let your body and brain relax for 10 to 30 minutes each day. Some people meditate, some look out of the window and others just close their eyes and relax. This time spent quietly will help you gain a clearer picture of what you want to achieve, and you may find that you have solved some of the problems you didn't have answers for by just being still
- Take care of yourself and build your energy. You can't concentrate if you are too tired, too lonely, too hungry or too thirsty
- Don't let your mind run on chaos. Remember everything is important, but not everything is urgent
- Self-observation, such as keeping a notebook, is an alternative to seeking out others. It offers some of the same benefits, including venting of feelings, distancing yourself from the situation, and increasing perspective of your goals. List your priorities
- During the day, if something comes into your mind, jot it down. Organize your thoughts this way. Doing this will free up the chaos your brain experiences when there's a lot on your mind. This simple task allows you to concentrate on one thing at a time, Keep the notebook with you at all times.

Remember, making changes in the way you think takes time and effort—don't give up on your road to creating a new you and a new healthy relationship with your partner.

8 | Implementing Change

Forgiving can be used as the first step when embarking on a journey of changing yourself in order to have a healthy relationship with your partner. While it is tempting to change everything about you all at once, in my experience if you do this you will confuse yourself and your partner. Your partner will wonder what you are about. Why you've changed. What you want. More importantly, has the change got anything to do with him/her? Your partner will become alert to the differences in you, and this will lead him/her to becoming suspicious of your intentions.

In order for long-term change to be successful, you have to discipline yourself and not be tempted by the "too much too soon" scenario. Changes need to be subtle, as they allow for a more positive and powerful outcome of the constant conflict you are experiencing.

There are different ways to change your ritual/routine, either by adding or removing patterns. Another simple and effective method of changing patterns is based on the rule, "Never engage in any activity unless you are able to tell at least two people of your intentions." If you are unable to do this, it is more likely that it is not a good thing for you to do. This rule is a kind of checklist that ensures your motives for the change is positive.

Negativity abounds when you are dealing with difficult situations. It permeates everything. It's important at this stage to examine your thoughts and to remember that it's the way you handle these thoughts that determines your mood and behavior. You may accept the thoughts in your mind as true and honest, but this is not always the case.

A good way to change a negative thought is to challenge its accuracy. You can do this by seeing the thought through someone else's eyes:

- Ask yourself how your parent would respond to the thought
- Ask yourself how your best friend would respond to the thought
- Ask yourself how the person you most admire would respond.

Thoughts that support beliefs about your strength, choice and optimism provide a basis for changes in attitudes, moods and behavior patterns. An essential part of creating a long-term strategy of change in your behavior pattern is to identify and change negative thought patterns.

Thoughts can be changed by first identifying them and then assessing their accuracy. This allows you to either dismiss each thought as of no real consequence or else choose to turn the thought around. All these methods will assist you in changing your thought patterns and subsequent behavior. It is important to identify, challenge and change your negative thought patterns. Changing your thoughts from negative to positive will help change your attitude, behavior and emotions.

- Negative thought—I am useless, I can't do anything.
- Positive thought—I am useful, I can do many things.

When you stop doing something that has been a life-long habit, it takes time, discipline and patience. If you are prepared to put in the effort, you will get a positive result. Of course, it is impossible to question every little thing you do. However, it pays to be open-minded and look at other ways to respond to your partner during conflicts.

Another simple change in behavior is to not respond to a question directly asked of you, and instead ask a question in return. In other words, throw the ball back to the other person/your partner. When quarrels occur, questions are asked, and the answers given are seen as important and vital to the outcome of the situation. So, if you give the wrong answer, the problem can get worse. However, if you answer the question with a non-judgmental question, you not only remove yourself from the confrontation of the moment, you may also defuse the situation.

- **Quarrel:** He says: "How do you see this relationship going?"
- She says: "I think it's all downhill—you don't listen to me or do anything I ask of you." (A typical response and one uttered by many).

By answering the question in this way you are adding fuel to the fire by challenging and criticizing your partner.

- **Quarrel:** He says: "How do you see this relationship going?"
- She says: "We have been together for a while, haven't we—how do you see the relationship?"

By using this approach and putting the ball firmly back in your partner's court, you are fact-finding to identify what he/she perceives as wrong in the relationship. By doing this you will know more of how your partner feels and, therefore, not only give a more satisfactory response but you will also have more time to think out how to answer. Your partner might respond by totally destroying the structure of your relationship. It is then up to you to decide if you want to go down that road or deflect his/her intention and mood by adopting a different stance. If, for instance your partner starts pulling your relationship apart, you could react by saying that you need time to think the issue through, as it's too important to discuss from the top of your head. Again, what you are doing is giving yourself and him/her more time. Moods change quite swiftly, and you could find that you will never need to answer the question. The time you have allowed to pass has diluted or dispersed the problem.

I have counseled many people who experience problems after their partner has been drinking or taken drugs. You will never resolve an issue when in this situation, so there's no point in having the discussion at this time. Far better to diffuse the situation by changing the subject or by giving stock banal answers until a more appropriate time when both of you are clear headed. I must state that, in my experience, spontaneous reactions in any circumstances can only lead to having more problems. So think carefully and clearly before you make rash statements. This is one small way you can change the outcome and empower yourself at the same time. What you are actually doing is taking control of the situation.

During this process, you will be observing yourself and your partner. The act of making one small change in your behavior will have an effect on your partner. Your partner won't be able to pinpoint the change, because it's too subtle. At first he/she might think they are imagining the change in you. Your partner will begin to see you differently. They might not like the change they see. In fact it's highly likely that they won't like the change, particularly if that one small change has a consequence for them. If you change one small thing about your reactions to situations, it has a catapult effect on your partner. He/she will have to change the way they respond to you. Generally people find any change in situations unsettling and confusing. Having made that one small change and by continually practicing this change in appropriate situations, do no more—just watch yourself and observe the responses of others.

Ask yourself:
- Did the situation turn around when you made that one small change?

- Did the situation stop when you made that one small change?
- Did it provoke an aggressive response?
- Did it provoke a more reasonable response?
- Did you feel in control of the situation?
- Did you feel out of control of the situation?
- Did you feel more able to continue the discussion after making the change?

These are some of the observations after making one small change in your behavior. Answer these questions honestly, and adapt your behavior according to the outcomes you have experienced. You could consider other responses. Sit down, think and write a few responses you could use in your notebook for future reference.

Changing behavior patterns for a more positive outcome in difficult situations is hard to achieve at first, but with practice it gets easier and your responses will become fluid and firmly established as a good habit. You must, however, take stock of your changing patterns from time to time. If you are happy that you have achieved a result with the one small change you have made, don't be tempted to make another yet. This is very important. You will be changing too quickly and too soon. In my experience, if you do this you will falter on your path of change and eventually give up trying. This time of observation is important to firmly establish your responses in difficult situations.

"The weak can never forgive. Forgiveness is the attribute of the strong."

Mahatma Gandhi

| 9 | **Consolidating Your Position** |

In my personal experience, it is important to take time between making changes to consolidate your newly found position—even though you might feel that does not amount to much of a change yet.

- You need "time out" to evaluate your position in your relationship
- You need "time out" to judge accurately if you are on the right road to changing
- You need "time out" to identify that the responses you made suit you and fit nicely within you.

This period of consolidation will help you to become more self-aware and will give you time to consolidate your new habit structures. You constantly need to reassess where you are and remember where you want to go. Don't forget that the steps you are taking lead you to your desired goal, which is a healthy new relationship after the decision and act of forgiveness.

During this time, reflect on difficult situations you have experienced since starting your action plan. If you have used your notebook correctly, you will have all the information you will need to accomplish this task. Go through your notebook, and remember the situations and difficulties you have gone through.

Ask yourself:

- Am I satisfied with my reactions at that time?

- Is there room for improvement?

In your mind, see yourself in the situation again, and change your response, trying something new and different, and imagine the outcome. Remember, no one knows their partner or family member better than you do. Open your mind to how you think your partner would react to the different changes you are contemplating before putting them into practice. If you think hard enough, you will know how your partner would respond to the changes you are experimenting with. All changes are difficult to make. To learn to change is a skill, and a skill is the ability to initiate, perform and complete difficult tasks. Make a habit of recording your achievements in your notebook. This simple, but disciplined, task will help you during the negative periods you will experience.

Having time to consolidate your new habits gives you a break from becoming totally absorbed in the changing process. Changing lifelong patterns is extremely tiring because you have to remain alert and focused at all times. You need this time of consolidation to give you time to "just be." Enjoy this time. You have adopted one small change to your pattern of behavior, and now you need to re-energize your mind and body, and you will accomplish this by relaxing. Learn to have quiet times. This is easier said than done. Read a novel, join an evening class, go for a drive in the car, go on a long walk, have a night out with friends or just take yourself off to your bedroom, lie down on the bed, close your eyes and think of something that makes you happy. Do something for you. Just relax into the moment.

Let's take a look at what you have achieved so far:
- You have learned to discipline your thoughts
- You have learned to forgive
- You have learned to accept responsibility

- You have learned how to identify your role in the conflict
- You have learned the difference between forgiving and forgetting
- You have learned how to devise a strategy
- You have learned how to devise an action plan
- You have learned how to implement your action plan
- You have learned to develop a reservoir of responses to assist you in resolving conflict
- You have learned to control your thoughts, reactions and behavior.
- You have learned not react
- You have learned to stay focused
- You have learned to reassess your situation
- You have learned how to eliminate negative repeating patterns
- You have learned to stop wasting your time and energy repeating the same strategy
- You have learned to explore other responses you could make in situations
- You have learned to practice your responses to situations
- You have learned to record your emotions and behavior in your notebook
- You have learned to evaluate the outcome you have achieved
- You have learned to be still within yourself and just simply "be."

These are twenty positive outcomes you have achieved in the forgiving process and on your journey of self-discovery.

I hope you can see the benefit of forgiving and turning your life around by using some of the methods and exercises I have outlined. One small change in your behavior is now well and truly part of your good habit strategy.

You took stock of your life by:

- Accepting your role in conflict situations
- Taking responsibility for yourself
- Being prepared to forgive your partner/others
- Using the "forgiving process" to change your negative repeating patterns of behavior
- Identifying what you wanted to change
- Preparing yourself to break lifelong patterns of behavior
- Not reacting spontaneously to situations
- Staying focused
- Developing a long term strategy
- Developing a short term strategy (achievable targets)
- Thinking through old responses
- Exploring and developing new ones
- Recording your emotions, thoughts and behavior in your notebook
- Practicing new habits
- Resisting the temptation inside you to change too much too soon
- Taking time out for yourself in order to re-energies
- Evaluating outcomes you achieved

When itemized in this wa,y you can see clearly how much you have achieved so far. Tick the items you feel you have achieved.

Your decision to forgive your partner/others has also triggered you to make profound changes in the way you are perceived by others and also the way you perceive yourself. You have made definitive steps in overcoming obstacles and have learned how to resolve conflicts.

You have embarked on a process to re-create your relationship with your partner and have also begun your personal voyage of self-discovery. None of these things would have been achievable if you had not accepted and decided to "forgive." You will continue to learn new things about yourself and your partner, and by using the exercises I have shown you, you will be able to adjust to the new habits. These adjustments you have undertaken in working with this book have required discipline, focus, effort and practice. You will also have learned to accept some setbacks as part of the process of learning new interactions and responses. The journey through this book is an emotional experience that is sometimes difficult to endure. The most important fact is that you didn't give up and have achieved some success.

10 | Your New Patterns of Behavior

This is the final step. Having worked through this process in order to find out more about "forgiving," you should now have established and accepted your action plan on the way to developing new patterns of behavior.

Your life's journey is often hard to deal with.

You will ask yourself these questions:
- "Why is this happening to me?"
- "What have I done to deserve this?"
- "Am I such a bad person?"
- "How can I change my life around?"

The answers to these questions is:
- It's happening to you because you have learned not to expect better
- You have done nothing wrong and don't deserve what is happening to you
- You are not a bad person
- You can change your life by focusing on new thoughts and ways to turn your life around
- You learn, early on in life, how to respond to different circumstances and situations.

You are conditioned by your role models and the environment you were raised in.

From this conditioning, you learn good and bad habits that take you through your life. This outcome cannot be avoided.

You are not responsible for the belief and behavior of your role models or for the environment you were raised in. You are, however, responsible and accountable for your beliefs, behavior and the environment you create for yourself today.

Don't look back and condemn or try to justify your past. Move on and create the life you deserve.

Marriage partnerships and friendships do not exist in a vacuum. A healthy relationship is built by both partners satisfying each other's emotional and physical needs. This means that each partner should engage in finding out what the other partner needs to be emotionally fulfilled. Without this knowledge, the relationship will be built on shifting sand and will be difficult to maintain. No relationship will be successful if only one partner is getting satisfaction. There will be times during the course of your relationship when one partner is being satisfied more than the other. This is a natural phenomenon. However, this should not be allowed to continue, as resentment will cause a barrier between you.

A healthy relationship should be based on a "win/win" intention. No one is taught how to create a healthy relationship. We all operate by "the seat of our pants" method. We all have learned our behavior and belief system on how to get along with people from our role models (parents, grandparents, aunts, uncles, foster care, children's homes, etc). Often, the role modeling we have absorbed is inappropriate and unsatisfying. Unfortunately, it is only when problems arise in our relationship do we seek to improve it. So what happens after you decide to improve your relationship? You start asking questions, surf the Internet to get answers, read self-help books, and/or confide in trusted family and friends. Or go to a suitable professional who will lead the two of you in improving your relationship.

Developing a healthy relationship doesn't have to be difficult. It can be and it has to be learned.

Here are the basic skills to develop a healthy relationship:
- Listening skills
- Understanding skills
- Empathy skills
- Common sense skills

Listening skills

You all have a right to be heard. You all have your own views on how things should be. You each have a right to say what you feel. The biggest compliment you can give your partner is listening to what he/she is saying. The way to make sure that your partner knows you are listening is to repeat back to your partner what he/she has said to you. I don't mean word for word. I mean a general statement back to your partner on the key issues he/she has raised.

Understanding skills

Learning to understand your partner's point of view can be difficult if you have strong views yourself on the issue being discussed. In order to forgive and move on, you must listen to what your partner is saying to you without interrupting him/her. When you do this, you are showing your partner that you value their input to the discussion. You are re-confirming to your partner that his/her views are important to you. Listen to what he/she says, and show your partner that you understand his/her point of view. When your partner has finished speaking you can then air your views on the subject being discussed. You will not always agree. This is normal. Sometimes you can agree to disagree, and other times you can both compromise and give each other at least some of things that you want. This is not rocket science. This interaction is fair and just, and should leave both partners feeling equal and valued.

Empathy skills

Learn the difference between sympathy and empathy. "Sympathy is the sharing of emotions, and empathy is identifying with another person's feelings." In a healthy relationship, there is both sympathy and empathy, and one should not be mixed up with the other. Showing your partner that you understand how he/she feels and giving an example of how you can identify his/her feelings will reassure your partner that your contribution to the issue raised is worth listening to. If you don't show your partner that you can identify with his/her feelings by giving an example of how you can link to his/her feelings, your partner will be unlikely to share his/her feelings with you—they will believe that because you have had no prior experience in the issue raised, you will not be able to contribute emotionally.

Common sense skills

Good old fashioned common sense never fails you. When the chips are down and you are fed up and confused analyzing issues between you and your partner, let common sense prevail. It won't let you down. Common sense is seated in truth, and it is not camouflaged with clever words aimed at confusing your opposing partner. If you have come to the conclusion that you cannot think straight, try the following exercise.

Try this exercise:

Think of three people you know who you believe are reasonable and mature adults. Next, ask the question you are worried about to each of these three individuals (in your mind, or written down). Next, answer the question as if you are each of these three individuals. If you do this exercise correctly, you will reach a satisfactory general option on how to resolve the problem.

Make a Safe Haven

Get to know your partner "warts and all." Develop your relationship so that it will become the "safe haven" in your life: the place you can retreat to when things outside your relationship are getting you down. Everyone needs and wants a safe haven. We all want to be cared for and loved. It's a natural emotional expectation. In the first instance, your safe haven might have been your parents' home or the home of a trusted friend, but as an adult your safe haven should be the home you share with your partner. Learn to trust your partner. Learn to share, communicate and be honest with your partner. Learn how to support your partner. Learn how to compromise with your partner. Learn to be part of a mutually satisfying relationship.

Forgive

Will you forgive me?
Is there a chance?
Can you forgive my misdeeds of the past?

I want your forgiveness
I will try to be good
To do all the right things
The way that I should

I should have known better
I should have known how
I made a mistake
God alone knows how!

I won't let you down
I promise to be true
If only you will let me
I will shine through

The judgment is over
The die has been cast
A decision to forgive me
Is all that I ask

Thank you my partner
My lover
My friend
Together united
We will be to the end

Lynda Bevan

Appendix A: Emergency Contacts

International Contacts:

1-800-THERAPIST (1-800-843-7274)	1-800-843-7274
Find-a-Therapist.com	1.866.450.3463
POWA Helpline	(011) 642-4345
The American Domestic Violence Crisis Line	866-USWOMEN

In Canada:

Assaulted Women's Helpline	416-863-0511
Domestic Violence Hotline	1-800-799-7233
National Domestic Violence Hotline	1-800-363-9010

In Australia:

Domestic Violence Crisis Hotline (NSW)	1800 656 463
Domestic Violence Crisis Hotline (Northern Territory)	1800 019 116
Domestic Violence Crisis Hotline (Queensland)	1800 811 811
Domestic Violence Crisis Hotline (South Australia)	1800 800 098
Domestic Violence Crisis Hotline (Tasmania)	1800 633 937
Domestic Violence Crisis Hotline (Victoria)	1800 007 339

In the United Kingdom:

Action on Elder Abuse Hotline	0808 808 8141
Muslim Women's Help Line	0181 904 8193
National Domestic Violence Hotline	0808 2000 247
Northern Ireland Women's Aid Federation	(028)90 31818

In the United States:

Asian Task Force against Domestic Violence Hotline	617-338-2355
Crisis Support Network	1-800-435-7276
National Domestic Violence Hotline	1-800-799-7233
Safe Horizon's Domestic Violence Hotline	800-621-4673
The American Domestic Violence Crisis Line	1-866-USWOMEN
The National Coalition Against Domestic Violence	303-839-1852

Bibliography

Allen, C. L. (2007). *Why good people make bad choices: How you can develop peace of mind through integrity.* Ann Arbor, MI: Loving Healing Press.

Amen, D. G. (1998). *Change your brain, change your life: The breakthrough program for conquering anxiety, depression, obsessiveness, anger, and impulsiveness.* New York: Times Books.

Brady, T. (2007). *Regaining control: When love becomes a prison.* Ann Arbor, MI: Loving Healing Press.

Covey, S. (1990). *The 7 habits of highly effective people.* A fireside book. New York: Simon & Schuster.

Davies, L. (1992) *Allies in healing: When the person you love was sexually abused as a child.* San Francisco: Harper Perennial

Goleman, D. (1995). *Emotional intelligence.* New York: Bantam Books.

Gray, J. (1998) *Men are from Mars, Women are from Venus.* Harper Collins

Jeffers, S. J. (1996). *End the struggle and dance with life: How to build yourself up when the world gets you down.* New York: St. Martin's Press.

Jeffers, S. (1997). *Feel the fear and do it anyway: How to turn your fear and indecision into confidence and action.* London: Rider.

Keith, K. M. (2002). *Anyway: The paradoxical commandments: finding personal meaning in a crazy world.* New York: Putnam.

Lew, M. (1990). *Victims no longer: Men recovering from incest and other sexual child abuse.* New York: Perennial Library.

McKenna, P., & Willbourn, H. (2006). *I can mend your broken heart.* London: Bantam.

Murphy, J. G. (2005). *Getting even: Forgiveness and its limits.* New York: Oxford University Press.

Norwood, R. (1985). *Women who love too much: When you keep wishing and hoping he'll change.* Los Angeles: J.P. Tarcher.

Norwood, R. (1994). *Why me, why this, why now: A guide to answering life's toughest questions.* New York: C. Southern Books

Pease, B., & Pease, A. (2000). *Why men don't listen & women can't read maps: How we're different and what to do about it.* New York, NY: Welcome Rain

Randall, P. (2001). *Bullying in adulthood: Assessing the bullies and their victims.* New York: Brunner-Routledge.

Volkman, M. (2005) *Life Skills: Improve the Quality of Your Life with Metapsychology.* Loving Healing Press: Ann Arbor, MI.

About the Author

Lynda Bevan lives in a picturesque village in South Wales, United Kingdom. She is 59 years of age, married for the third time, with three (adult) children. During her teens and early twenties, she pursued and enjoyed acting and taught drama at local Youth Centers.

Her 22-year career has involved working in the area of mental health, with the two major care agencies in the UK, Social Services and the National Health Service.

After the birth of her third child, and with her second marriage ending, she became employed by Social Services and climbed through the ranks to senior management level with some speed.

During her career with Social Services, she developed a passion for counseling and psychotherapy and worked extensively with mental health patients within the organization, setting up counseling projects in Healthcare Centers. The task was to tackle the issue of doctors who inappropriately referred patients to Psychiatric Hospitals for therapy when they had experienced events that arise in normal everyday life, e.g., divorce, anxiety, depression, bereavement, stress, loss of role. It was during this time that she became involved in marital/relationship counseling and, coincidentally, was experiencing difficulties within her own relationship. The experience of working in this environment, and her own relationship issues, enabled Lynda to be innovative; creating

methods of coping and developing strategies that enabled her and her patients to live within their problematic relationships. These strategies were devised and offered to patients who had clearly identified that they did not want to separate or proceed with the divorce process.

After taking early retirement from Social Services, she became employed by the National Health Service as a Counselor in the Primary Healthcare Setting. During this period in her career, she began using the strategies she had developed with patients who were referred for relationship counseling and who did not want to end their partnership/ marriage. These strategies have been used extensively over a ten-year period with impressive results.

Lynda is presently employed as a Manager of a charity that supports people who are HIV positive. She is also the Resident Relationship Counselor on Swansea Sound Radio.

Index

www.ingramcontent.com/pod-product-compliance
Lightning Source LLC
LaVergne TN
LVHW091200080426
835509LV00006B/767